4
ABUNDANT LIFE

4 ABUNDANT LIFE

4 Biblical Truths to Experience a Life of Abundance

DRS. ERIC & JOANNA OESTMANN

WESTBOW
PRESS
A DIVISION OF THOMAS NELSON

WestBow Press books may be ordered through booksellers or by contacting:

WestBow Press
A Division of Thomas Nelson
1663 Liberty Drive
Bloomington, IN 47403
www.westbowpress.com
1-(866) 928-1240

All Scripture quotes are from the New International Version
(NIV) Bible unless otherwise specified in text.

ISBN: 978-1-4497-8436-2 (sc)
ISBN: 978-1-4497-8437-9 (hc)
ISBN: 978-1-4497-8435-5 (e)

Library of Congress Control Number: 2013902284

Printed in the United States of America

WestBow Press rev. date: 2/8/2013

CONTENTS

Introduction

What took us nearly forty years to learn about the abundant life promise we would like to share with you in less than four hours. Yes, it should take you only about an hour to read each of the four sections in this book.

First, we hope that you picked up this book because you want to experience a life of abundance. Simply stated, you would like *more* in your life than you currently have. If this desire resonates with you, relax. We are all born with this desire, and it is what our God wants for us too!

One of the first words we learn to say is *more*. Think back to your earliest childhood memories of a favorite food or drink. Did you want more of it? Of course you did. Did your parents give you more of it? Of course they did … to the point of not harming you.

This same analogy applies to the parent/child relationship between our heavenly Father and us (His children). After all, how much more does He care about us than the birds of the field, and yet He provides for them too?

The Gift of Abundance

He cared so much that He gave His only Son to cancel the debt of our sin and allow us to live eternally in heaven! The greatest gift our Father could ever give, He gave us. We did not earn it, and we certainly do not deserve it. Hence, the definition of a gift!

And those who accept the truth receive the gift of salvation. However, the gift is more than just eternal peace. In fact, the Lord's Prayer includes "on earth as it is in heaven," verbiage that is directly related to the promise of abundance declared by Jesus in John 10:10, NIV: "...I have come that they may have life, and have it abundantly."

Heaven on earth sounds pretty abundant to us. In fact, there have been dozens of self-help books written over the years on the topic of abundance. An equal number of seminars and programs have also been promoted to help individuals experience *more* in their lives. Millions have read the books, attended the seminars, spent money on the programs, and yet failed to experience a life of abundance.

Why?

The short answer starts with the fact that we all have blind spots that prevent us from seeing the scope and magnitude of the abundance gift. If we cannot see it, we cannot know what we are entitled to ask for and receive. Consequently, most who fail to live in abundance have a blind spot that limits the gift to the eternal hereafter. In other words, we do not see the gift of abundance (our *birthright inheritance* through Jesus Christ, our Lord and Savior) here on earth.

That said, we must first accept and believe that everything written in the Bible is true. (According to 2 Timothy 3:16, "All Scripture is God-breathed.") Alternatively, nothing in the Bible is true and we can simply close the book now. In short, we cannot pick and choose what we like or believe from biblical Scripture. It is an all or nothing proposition!

We assume you have chosen to believe that everything in the Bible is true or you would not have kept reading. The great news for those who believe that the Bible is true, and accept Jesus as the Son of God who took on the sin of the world for us, is that this entitles us to the gift. We have become children of God. (Galatians 3:26: "In Christ Jesus you are all children of God.") As a child, we are given an inheritance from our Father.

Obviously, God thought we should know something about an inheritance. In fact, more than two hundred Bible verses discuss inheritance. As we all know, an inheritance is a gift not dependent on works. (Galatians 3:18: "For if the inheritance depends on the law, then it no longer depends on the promise.")

Think about it in earthly terms. An inheritance is gifted to us while we are alive by a family member who loved us and passed through the pearly gates. That inheritance is designed to help us during our remaining time on earth. In other words, an inheritance is something we can use *right now* in order to experience a more abundant life.

Our inheritance is most definitely intended for good use while we are on this side of the grass. (Matthew 5:5: "Blessed are the meek/humble, for they will inherit the earth.") Inheriting the earth implies a pretty big blessing. The promise did not say, "You will inherit *some* of the earth." The promise included the *whole* earth and everything in it. In fact, the law of abundance is one of the principles that govern the universe, like the law of gravity, because there is an unlimited Source of everything we need or could ever want. That Source, of course, is our Father in heaven, and we are the beneficiaries of the inheritance of abundance. (Ephesians 3:20: "Now to Him who is able to do immeasurably more than all we ask or imagine.")

It is unfortunate that our English translation has lost some of the richness of the original Greek, Latin, and Hebrew Scriptures. *Meek/humble* does not mean the person is as quiet as a church-mouse or a pushover. A meek/humble person is one who follows instructions without question. In other words, they are faithful and obedient to God's word, according to Emmet Fox.[1]

It is also important here not to apply a legalistic standard of performance perfection regarding the conditional terms *faithful* and *obedient*. (Romans

3:23: "For all have sinned and fall short.") In other words, we cannot always be faithful and obedient, and the good news is that God already knows this but accepts us anyway. Religious rules and performance standards have made a relationship with Christ more difficult than it was ever intended to be. When we live by rules and performance, we make our blind spots bigger and limit our inheritance of abundance.

When you feel like you do not deserve a blessing because of your failures, just remember that your failures are never final. Know that you are in good company, as we all fall short. Believe that God's *grace* (getting a gift we do not deserve) is bigger than any sin!

RECAP

Do you understand what the abundant life promise is?

I think so …

As a faithful and obedient child of God (believer in Christ Jesus), I am entitled to an inheritance. It may be anything God chooses to give me (possibly as big as the entire earth) that I can use right now in order to help me live an abundant life. This is a promise in the Bible, and I believe all of it to be true.

Yes!

So when will He turn the inheritance faucet of abundant blessings on?

Good question. We are glad you asked. The 4 Abundant Life experience is grounded in four biblical truths:

1. **We (children of God, Christ followers) are anointed to prosper**

2. **At an appointed time and place,**

3. **When we use our talents and gifts,**

4. For the glory of Him!

Experiencing a life of abundance is as easy, and as challenging, as that!

The rest of the book is organized according to each of the four truths that include Scriptures, supporting stories, personal experiences, word pictures, and reflective questions for application. We hope you find this book to be as much a blessing to read as it was for us to write and share with the world.

PART 1

We Are Anointed to Prosper!

"For I know the plans I have for you," declares the LORD, "plans to prosper you and not to harm you, plans to give you hope and a future."

Jeremiah 29:11

CHAPTER 1

4 Abundant Life: The Number Four

THE BIBLE IS FULL OF meaningful numbers like three—Triune God (Father, Son, and Spirit) and Threefold cord (love, faith, and hope)—and twelve (number of apostles and number of months in a year).

So what about the number four?

There are four seasons (winter, spring, summer, and fall). There are four directions (north, south, east, and west). There are four elements (earth, wind, fire, and water). One of Jesus' first miracles was feeding four thousand people with a few loaves of bread and fish. In another miracle, Lazarus was raised from the dead after four days. Four books in the New Testament chronicle the Jesus story (Matthew, Mark, Luke, and John). It parallels the reference to the four living creatures at the center of the heavenly throne in Revelation, where Matthew is the human face, Mark is the lion face, John is the eagle face, and Luke is the ox face. While each author tells the same story, one might think only one book would be needed. However, God thinks differently from how we think. There is a purposeful intention that the Jesus story is told four different times by four different authors. The number four has long been associated with completion, stability, and predictability.

We know Jesus was a carpenter by trade. No doubt, He constructed a table or two in His days while apprenticing under His earthly father Joseph. As we all know, tables will not stand without all four legs being of equal length sitting on a firm foundation. A four-legged table is our word picture that represents the *4 Abundant Life* inheritance promise.

THE FOUNDATION

Build your table on the firm foundation of Jesus Christ!

Luke 6:46–48: Why do you call me, "Lord, Lord," and do not do what I say? As for everyone who comes to me and hears my words and puts them into practice, I will show you what they are like. They are like a man building a house, who dug down deep and laid the foundation on rock. When a flood came, the torrent struck that house but could not shake it, because it was well built. But the one who hears my words and does not put them into practice is like a man who built a house on the ground without a foundation. The moment the torrent struck that house, it collapsed and its destruction was complete.

If you think you have done too many bad things in life to ever be forgiven for them, you are wrong! In fact, pay attention to the verb tense in Colossians 2:13: "He forgave us all our sins." Yes, that is *forgave*—past tense—which includes all sins (past, present, and future).

2 Corinthians 5:17: "Therefore, if anyone is in Christ, the new creation has come: The old has gone, the new is here!"

If you are not a believer and follower of Jesus Christ, it is never too late.

John 3:16: "For God so loved the world that he gave his one and only Son, that whoever believes in him shall not perish but have eternal life."

If you believe in your heart and confess with your mouth, you should be confident that heaven is your eternal resting place. In other words, you can build your abundant life table on the firm foundation of Jesus Christ constructed of four table legs.

THE FOUR TABLE LEGS

1. **We (children of God, Christ followers) are anointed to prosper**
    The inheritance gift of abundance is one of the table legs. Understanding the scope of the gift is central to experiencing a life of abundance and avoiding the blind spots that limit the gift as we discussed in the introduction. This will be discussed in much greater detail in chapters 2 and 3.

2. **At an appointed time and place,**
    There are three conditions applied to receiving and living the inheritance gift of abundance. A time and place exist for every good gift that represents another table leg. This will be discussed in chapters 4, 5, and 6.

3. **When we use our talents and gifts,**
    Another condition applied to experiencing the abundant life is based on the table leg of using our talents and gifts. An important caveat in this section is grounded in living an authentic life intended by God at the time of creation. More on these topics will be shared in chapters 7, 8, and 9.

4. **For the glory of Him!**
    We are representatives of the Most High God! Upon receiving

gifts of abundance, we are able to share our blessings with others to provide glory to the Giver. Miracles of reconciliation and redemption will reinforce this representation of the abundant life table leg in chapters 10, 11, and 12.

THE TABLE TOP

The blessings of abundance are represented by gifts presented to us on top of the table word picture. Of course, the Enemy would like nothing more than to steal your gift and replace it with trouble (a rock word picture).

Because our lives on earth are fraught with sin, there will be *trouble rocks* placed on top of our table of abundance.

> John 16:33: "In this world you will have trouble ... But take heart! I have overcome the world."

We all experience troubles in life. However, the abundant life table with four equal legs is able to withstand the rocks that life piles on. This is contrasted with the word picture that occurs when one or more of the abundant life table legs are shorter than the others and trouble rocks are piled on.

AVOIDING UNBALANCE

The Enemy uses a very common weapon to shorten our abundant life table legs and throw us off balance. We should recognize and avoid the weapon of *performance* in order to maintain our balanced table that will withstand trouble rocks as they come and go.

We both grew up in the church (Eric: Lutheran; Joanna: Catholic). We both went to church on Sunday because that is what you did as children and later as adults and as parents. However, neither of us experienced a *living church* during these formative years. The messages and music never really spoke to us. We were more excited about what was for lunch after church than the service itself. But one thing stuck with us from all those Sundays, and it centered on a performance theme:

"You're going to hell if you don't _____ (fill in the blank of performance)."

Ultimately, this led to a life of uncertainty and imbalance. We were not certain if our goods outweighed our bads in life. We were not certain our names would be in the Book of Life. We were not certain we would be able to answer the questions to enter the pearly gates guarded by St. Peter. By definition, we were lukewarm Christians, or casual Christians. However, this uncertainty was not the fault of the Lutheran, Catholic, or any other denomination church. It simply was our reality based on our knowledge and experiences at that time.

GET OFF THE PERFORMANCE TREADMILL!

If your performance drives your confidence in the hereafter, you can change that viewpoint. Jesus Himself gave us the instruction when he taught us to pray the Lord's Prayer. Specifically, the verse below explains this concept by which you cannot out-sin God's grace.

> Matthew 6:13 "And lead us not into temptation, but deliver us from the evil one."

REMEMBER ...

The two traps/temptations Jesus instructs us to avoid are to believe that:

1. **Everything is a sin.**

2. **Nothing is a sin.**

Where do these temptations come from? Yes, the evil one (Matthew 6:13). If you think everything is a sin, performance and guilt will dictate your life and keep you from experiencing abundance. If you think nothing is a sin, frivolity and callousness will dictate your life and keep you from experiencing abundance. Assuming either preposition is true will *not* deliver you from the Evil One.[1]

Just like the legs on our abundant life table, if one is longer/shorter than the others, the table is out of balance and easily tipped over by trouble rocks in life. Rather, we are instructed by virtue of the Lord's Prayer to seek balance by avoiding these temptations.

Remember the success principle "What you focus on expands!"

If we focus too much on sin, what do you do? That's right; we sin. We are all wired with this subconscious influence on behavior. Even the apostle Paul struggled with focusing too much on sin.

Romans 7:15 "I do not understand what I do. For what I want to do, I do not do, but what I hate to do."

Recognizing this imbalanced focus Paul went on to write,

Romans 7:17 "As it is, it is no longer I myself who do it [sin], but it is sin living in me."

God's grace covers all sin. In other words, we cannot out-sin Gods grace. And for some of us we have tried, a lot!

The average human sins, conservatively, at least twenty times a day (in thought, word, or deed) x 365 days a year for an average lifespan of seventy years. That is more than half a million (511,000) sins in a lifetime!

However, anyone (which includes *you*) who believes in Christ is forgiven of all sins, past, present, and future. As far as the east is from the west, your sins are remembered no more.

Acts 13:38 "Therefore, my friends, I want you to know that through Jesus the forgiveness of sins is proclaimed to you."

Think about It! Do you still feel inadequate? Not forgiven? Like you haven't done enough to tip the scale on the "good deeds" side to counterbalance your sin? Does everything feel like a sin?

If you answered *yes* to any of the above questions, it is normal. However, it is also an incorrect feeling or belief that limits an abundant life.

We live in a performance based and driven culture where more is better. The harder we try to work, the more we should be recognized and rewarded for that effort. However, we should think about Dysmas, the sinner on the cross next to Jesus. Before Dysmas died on that cross, he gave his life to Christ and Christ assured him he would be with Him in heaven.

Dysmas was good enough for Christ even though he was a lifelong criminal and sinner. He was an unbeliever until the final moments of his earthly life, he did not tithe a penny to the church, and in fact, he never attended church. He probably did not do many kind things at all in his life, and yet because he believed, he was forgiven and given a life of eternity in heaven.

Had Dysmas met Christ and accepted Him earlier in life, it is most certain he would have experienced a much more joyful and abundant life than he did.

Be mindful that accepting Christ is not a license to sin! We should always keep that balance between: (a) *Everything is a sin* – performance; versus (b) *Nothing is a sin* – free pass. We are after all called to demonstrate works (i.e., put forth some effort to make the world a little better than it was when we got here). And one of the most misunderstood passages of the Bible, James 2:17 "Faith by itself, if it does not have works, is dead" needs further explanation.

Many use this verse independent of the preceding and post-ceding verses. Many think this verse supports the performance driven basis of salvation. However, salvation cannot be earned. Salvation is a gift to be accepted. You cannot pay for a gift, or it is no longer a gift.

First of all, James is writing to believers in Christ. Believers are anointed with the Holy Spirit and already saved. James 2:14 uses the word *profit* intentionally. Works done for the glory of Christ (i.e., that display faith) will profit a person (i.e., joyful and abundant life) now and more importantly as part of our heavenly reward (i.e., judgment seat of Christ) if they are done in context with the conditions (i.e., legs of the abundant life table):

At an appointed time and place,
When we use our talents and gifts,
For the glory of Him!

But first, let's explore the anointing promise; our birthright inheritance more fully.

RECAP

Think about It! What was the most recent trouble rock you experienced? Did you feel like your life was in balance or out of balance? What did you do first when you experienced the trouble? Pray? Swear? Drink? Use Drugs? Turn to Pornography? _____Other?

_____

_____

_____

_____

REMEMBER ...

The good news is that you can always rebuild and rebalance your four table legs to experience the abundant life. He has overcome the world and always will. And what we have learned along the way has allowed us *all* the right to experience a joyful and abundant life. God really does want to give you an abundant life. Dream big! Dream bigger! Your inheritance is more than you can imagine!

CHAPTER 2

The Anointing Promise: Our Inheritance

*A*s SPECIFIED IN THE INTRODUCTION, the Anointing Promise is based on the premise that we are children of God through the acceptance of Jesus Christ as His Son. Based on this birthright, we are anointed with the Holy Spirit (blessed and chosen to receive an inheritance) from our Father.[2] It is a promise that does *not* require performance or perfection. (Galatians 3:18: "For if the inheritance depends on the law, then it no longer depends on the promise.")

There are two components to the anointing promise.

First, there is the inheritance of eternal life in heaven once our names are written in the Book of Life (Revelation 3:5: "I will never blot out the name of that person from the book of life, but will acknowledge that name before my Father and his angels.") *Never* is a promise of Jesus you can count on, and *eternity* is a mighty long time!

Second, there is an inheritance of joyful and abundant life here on earth that is promised to us (John 10:10, Amp: "The thief comes only in order to steal and kill and destroy. I came that they may have *and* enjoy life, and have it in abundance (to the full, till it overflows))."

Joy and Abundance

Christ promises us a joyful and abundant life.

Do we all want to enjoy life? Do we all want to have an abundant life?

I think it is safe to say the universal answer is *yes*. But do we actually experience joyful and abundant life?

Hopefully, the answer is at least *sometimes*.

Joy

Joy is sometimes confused with happiness. Joy is long lasting whereas happiness is momentary. Joy comes from within us and is not tied to our circumstances. Happiness is often tied to what happens around us. Joy is a fruit (gift) of the Holy Spirit given to all believers.

Ephesians 5:22: "The fruit of the Spirit is love, joy, peace, forbearance, kindness, goodness, faithfulness, gentleness, and self-control."

With the gift of joy, people can experience joy, even if the circumstances around them create unhappiness. In other words, there can be joy even in difficult situations. For example, the death of a loved one is nearly always a difficult, stressful time. However, those who believe can also experience joy. It is the joy of knowing our loved one is in heaven, where there is no pain or suffering, tears or crying, and he or she will be waiting for us while praying and watching over us in the meantime.

Think about It! Reflect on the last time you had an absolutely fantastic moment, day, or week. What made it so blissful? How did you feel? Was it joy or happiness?

ABUNDANCE

Abundance is often confused with greed. Abundance is our natural birthright, or inheritance, as children of God to have our every need met and exceeded. However, greed is simply not being satisfied or content with abundance. Greed is also related to happiness. Greedy people, in addition to people with low self-worth, seek happiness through material goods and use material wealth to influence others. And we are instructed to be on guard against all kinds of greed (Luke 12:15).

So what exactly is the abundant life Jesus talks about?

Ephesians 3:20: "Now to Him who is able to do immeasurably more than all we ask or imagine, according to His power that is at work within us."

Abundance is therefore more than we could ask or imagine. The only limitation is that abundance does not become greed, and it must be used to glorify Him.

Luke 16:10: "Whoever can be trusted with very little can also be trusted with much, and whoever is not trusted (dishonest) with very little will also be dishonest with much."

Abundance is often categorized into tangible and intangible categories.

1. Tangible abundance may be a newer or bigger house or car, another child, a spouse with a kinder, gentler spirit, a more fulfilling job, etc.

2. Intangible abundance may be a feeling of security, enjoying the little things, having peace and feelings of respect, etc.

Think about It! What does an abundant life mean and look like to you?

The introduction discussed the inheritance gift of abundance in some detail. It is important to remember that our inheritance is most definitely intended for good use while we are on this side of the grass, which includes the *whole* earth and everything in it.

As we reflect on what a joyful and abundant life looks, feels, smells, and tastes like, the question we often ask ourselves is this: Why don't we experience more of this joyful and abundant life?

The short answer is grounded in the fact that we all too often create our own limitations or restrictions on the abundant inheritance. Let's examine this further in chapter 3.

RECAP

Think about It! How does your *joyful and abundant life* day begin, progress, and end? Where are you? What are you doing? Who are you with? What is around you? What are you seeing, smelling, tasting, touching, and hearing?

_____

_____

_____

_____

REMEMBER ...

Our inheritance for a joyful and abundant life is available to us right now! As a faithful and obedient child of God (believer in Christ Jesus), *you* are entitled to an inheritance that may be anything God chooses to give (possibly as big as the entire earth) that you can use right now in order to help you live an abundant life. This is a promise in the Bible, and I believe all of it to be true. We are *all* anointed to prosper!

CHAPTER 3

Recognize and Avoid Limitations

In chapter 2, we briefly examined the anointing promise of an abundant life and what that looks like in terms of joy and abundance. However, we often limit the scope and magnitude of our inheritance blessings by applying legalistic standards of performance perfection (i.e., everything is a sin). When we live by rules and performance, we make our blind spots bigger and limit our inheritance of abundance vision. Some additional limitations we need to recognize and avoid involve common human conditions, such as the following.[3, 4, 5]

1. We think small.

2. We use incorrect self-talk and do not embrace change.

3. We focus too much on the negative.

4. We are hedonistic by nature, seeking pleasure and avoiding pain.

Thinking Small

The story of Mr. Jones is a good illustration of thinking small.[6]

> Mr. Jones dies and goes to heaven. Peter is waiting at the gates to give him a tour. Amid the splendor of the golden streets, beautiful mansions, and choirs of angels, Mr. Jones notices an odd-looking building. He thinks it looks like an enormous warehouse. But when he asks to see inside, Peter hesitates. "You really don't want to see what's in there," he tells the new arrival. But Mr. Jones wonders why there would be any secrets in heaven. So when the tour is over, Mr. Jones asks again to see inside the structure.

> Finally, Peter relents.

> When the door is opened, Mr. Jones almost knocks Peter over in his haste to enter. It turns out that the enormous building is filled with row and row of shelves, floor to ceiling, each stacked neatly with white boxes tied in red ribbons.

> "These boxes all have names on them," Mr. Jones muses aloud. Then turning to Peter he asks, "Do I have one?"

> "Yes, you do." Peter tries to guide Mr. Jones back outside. But Mr. Jones is already dashing toward the "J" aisle to find his box.

> Peter follows, shaking his head. He catches up with Mr. Jones just as he is slipping the red ribbon off his box and popping the lid. Looking inside, Jones has a moment of instant recognition, and he lets out a deep sigh like the ones Peter has heard so many times before.

> Because in Mr. Jones' white box are all the blessings

that God wanted to give to him while he was on earth, but Mr. Jones never asked for them.

....

Matthew 21:22: "If you believe, you will receive whatever you ask for in prayer."

....

Think about It! Based on the Scripture from Matthew, if we ask for little blessings, we receive little blessings. However, if we ask for big blessings, we will receive big blessings. What does an abundant life look like from God's perspective? What are we missing out on? What did you last ask your Father for? Was it something small or something *big*?

WRITE IT DOWN

It is also important to consider writing down your requests for blessings of abundance on a regular basis. Make two columns. The first one is titled "Ask God For" and the second is "Thank God For." You will also be encouraged to see the prayer requests answered over time, which will also allow you to share your blessing testimonies with others. If you can dream it, you can become it or achieve it and experience it to the fullest. Just be open to what His thoughts may be to manifest the blessing in your life.

I THOUGHT VERSUS MY THOUGHTS

Any place in the Bible where a character is talking about a situation that begins with "I thought ..." there is an inevitable dialogue that describes something entirely different, showing us that God thinks differently than we do. His thoughts are higher than our thoughts. His ways are different from our ways.[7] (Isaiah 55:8: "For My thoughts are not your thoughts, neither are your ways my ways, declares the Lord.")

For example, Naaman, the commander of Aram's army (2 Kings 5), had contracted the disease of leprosy. Naaman was given the command to be healed by the prophet Elisha. Naaman traveled a great distance to see Elisha, and when he arrived, Elisha did not even come out to greet the commander. Rather, Elisha sent a servant to instruct Naaman to wash seven times in the Jordan River (a notoriously dirty river). Angry and leaving in a rage, Naaman went away saying, "I thought that he would surely come out to me and stand and call on the name of the Lord his God, wave his hand over the spot and cure me of my leprosy" (2 Kings 5:11). Later, Naaman did what Elisha instructed, having nothing to lose. "So he went down and dipped himself in the Jordan seven times and his flesh was restored and became clean like that of a young boy" (2 Kings 5:14). Upon receiving that miracle, Naaman exclaimed, "Now I know that there is no God in all the world except in Israel" (2 Kings 5:15).

What we know from this story is that Naaman expected a miracle to occur according to his own thoughts. But God had a different plan, a different perspective, and higher thoughts. A seemingly contradictory set of instructions to bathe in a dirty river only to emerge healed from leprosy with the skin of a young boy. Not just restoration, but abundant healing occurred!

What we know from this and many other stories in the Bible is that we limit God's intended blessing of abundance by having preconceived ideas of how our prayers should be answered. Preconceived thoughts block our ability to think with emotional intelligence. Then, when *what we thought would happen* does not occur, anger commonly results. Anger steals the joy from our lives and runs counter to living abundantly. However, if we can open ourselves up to His will, His thoughts, and His plans and shift from an *I thought* to a *My thought* mind-set, God will open the faucet of blessings upon us.[8]

Consider another Old Testament example made popular in recent years by Bruce Wilkinson's book *The Prayer of Jabez*.[6] For context, Jabez' name was part of his problem of not experiencing an abundant life until he prayed a specific and now very well-known prayer. Jabez' name meant "pain," and we can only surmise that he had a very large head, hence his mother's insistence for the child's name. However, Jabez knew how to accept God's blessings, whatever they might be.

1 Chronicles 4:10: "Oh that you would bless me indeed and enlarge my territory! Let your hand be with me, and keep me from harm so that I will be free from pain. And God granted his request."

Jabez didn't tell God how to bless him, enlarge his territory, or keep him from harm and pain. He simply trusted God would know best how to do it. And God did!

Many times, people will blame or curse God for not answering their prayers. But one must ask about what they prayed for first. Was it small, specific, concrete, and myopic? Did it limit the acknowledgment and authority of God's abundance options?

It is vitally important that we do not put God in a small box, or a big box for that matter. God does not fit in any box. He created the universe and His resources are endless! *Letting go and letting God* is a great slogan, but often it is difficult for us to do. And yet *Faith math* (adds power, subtracts weakness, divides difficulties, multiplies possibilities) helps us always remember that God has plans for our good and that His thoughts are always higher than our thoughts.

AUTHOR'S PERSONAL MEANING OF THE NUMBER 4

The number four has specific meaning and significance to us that is directly related to letting go and letting God, thinking *big,* and waiting to see what *My Thoughts* would look like. After both of us were divorced and single for four years, without successful dating prospects, we finally acquiesced to God's will. We opened ourselves up to accepting a blessing according to His will instead of our own will. A simple prayer was spoken by each of us, something like this: "God, I give up trying to find the one to make me whole again. You are more than enough for me, and I trust in you." It was one of the few times in life where we let go and let God.

Proverbs 3:5–6: "Trust in the Lord with all your heart. Lean not on your own understanding. But in all ways acknowledge Him and He will direct your paths."

Being 2,500 miles apart (Eric in South Dakota and Joanna in Florida), these prayers were heard and answered. The path directed to Chicago.

At a once-in-a-lifetime conference in Chicago, we met face-to-face, and four days later, on 4–4–2004, at 4 p.m., with an outside temperature of 44 degrees, there was no doubt about it. We were in love and meant to be. Married shortly thereafter, we blended our children and experienced the abundant life God promises all of us. Now that is not to say we did not also experience troubles (i.e., rocks) along the way. But with the abundance table built on the firm foundation of Christ, we have been able to withstand trouble rocks and thrive through the awesome power of reconciliation and redemption. More on this in the final section of the book. Until then, one way to help refrain from limiting God's blessings is to evaluate and change our self-talk.

Think about It! When was the last time you limited the blessing from God? Was it based on an *I thought* perspective or reflection?

SELF-TALK AND CHANGE

The definition of *insanity* is simply defined as "doing the same thing over and over again, expecting, but not experiencing, different results." However, change for the sake of change is not a growth opportunity.

Over the years, we have experienced this with many organizations that change things for no reason other than "it is time for a change." However, is there a need for the change? That should be the question we always ask first. When there is a good reason for change, then we should proactively embrace that change.

First, be mindful that all humans naturally resist change. Our subconscious wiring is a servomechanism that likes the status quo.

The only way to override the subconscious is through conscious self-talk substitution of the words *have to* and *need to* with *want to* and *choose to*.

The words we speak have power and influence over the blessings, or lack thereof, in our lives. (Proverbs 18:21: "The tongue has the power of life and death.")

Pay attention to your self-talk. If you hear yourself say out loud, "I have to mow the yard today," your subconscious already told your inner brain, "No, you don't." It is where procrastination comes from.

However if you change your self-talk to, "I choose to mow the yard today so I have time to take my daughter fishing," your subconscious can't resist it. You have made a conscious choice that overrides the resistance.[9, 10, 11] I want to, I choose to, I like to, I love to overrides the subconscious resistance and gives you power, choice, and sustained change.

CHANGE IS NECESSARY FOR GROWTH!

Matthew 18:3: "Truly I tell you, unless you change and become like little children, you will never enter the kingdom of heaven."

Ever wonder why Jesus said this? What does it mean?

Jesus is asking us to enter the kingdom like little children running to their heavenly Father, not worried about doing enough good things to get in the door. Children know it is their house when they enter. They don't have to pay for the house. Jesus already did that!

Perhaps the following example will help further illustrate the point related to being anointed to prosper.

Do you remember a happy time in your childhood? A time of playing, riding bikes, shooting baskets with friends, reading, or eating ice cream without a care in the world? You were confident that your parents would feed you, cloth you, and put a roof over your head. You weren't worried about rent, utilities, or repair bills; where your next meal would come from; or if you would have clothes to wear. You simply lived life carefree.

If you didn't experience a moment in time where life was carefree, close your eyes and pretend you are five years old. You are told you get to go on a vacation to Disney World and you are flying on an airplane to get there. You are totally excited and you are first to board the plane. You are not told which seat you have to sit in. Rather, you can sit anywhere you want. Where do you sit?

First class, of course!

The front row (first on/first off), bigger seats, free snacks, all the juice you can drink, a private bathroom that you can actually stand up in … Yeah! That is what we are talking about with regard to abundance and childlike faith. You are unashamed, innocent, and untainted. You can be anything you want to be when you grow up: astronaut, fire fighter, lawyer, doctor, nurse—anything!

So why is it so hard for us adults to have childlike faith and dream big?

Simply put, life inevitably happens and deflates the helium balloon of childlike faith. Our expectations about an abundant life get replaced with earthly realities. Those trouble rocks accumulate and weigh us down. Our abundant life table becomes unsteady and burdened with the rocks of life.

But God does not place a time limit on receiving an abundant life. It is not only for kids.

The good news about change is that Jesus promises to help us change. Here are some helpful hints for adopting change in yourself:[5, 14]

1. Examine – What do you want changed?

2. Explore – I wonder what it would be like to …?

3. Experiment – Try it out on a small scale.

4. Make a Decision – Stay the same, change, or keep exploring.

5. Make a Commitment – Support the changes or go back

and get more information from examining, exploring, and experimenting.

6. Let Go of the Old – Don't hang on to the past.

7. Live in the present, the here, and now – Life is a "present" we give to ourselves.

Think about It! For the next day, week, and month, count the number of times you or your significant other says, "have to" or "need to" versus "want to" or "choose to." Is there a change? How has that change impacted your experience of the joyful and abundant life?

WHAT WE FOCUS ON EXPANDS

Whether positive or negative, what we focus on expands. If we focus on problems and worries, they get bigger. Therefore, it is essential to make the negative things as small as possible. Speak them into *iota* status. Iota is the smallest letter of the Greek alphabet, a speck. Keep the problems and worries small. If you don't, those problems and worries will get in the way of receiving God's blessings of abundance.

Regret and guilt! We all make mistakes, but keep them in perspective. They serve as a reminder for us to make better choices, but like the purpose of a rear-view mirror in a car, we cannot move the car forward (without crashing) if we are forever focused on the past (rear-view mirror).[12] Mistakes are good! They give us time to reflect and remember that nobody is perfect, including ourselves. Our mistakes or bad choices are all learning opportunities to help us grow and become better people. So instead of asking ourselves, "What did I do wrong?" we should be asking, "What would I do differently next time?" or "What is the lesson to be learned from this?" These questions allow us to focus forward and become excited about new opportunities for changing our behavior the next time.

Matthew 6:34: "Do not worry about tomorrow, for tomorrow will worry about itself."

If you are not familiar with the concept of appreciative inquiry (AI)—what is right with the world or the glass is half-full perspective—there are a lot of resources to review. We highly recommend the videos by *National Geographic* photographer Dewitt Jones (http://www.youtube.com/watch?v=xYTBTz2W3s8). A book written in the 1900s by James Allen, entitled *As a Man Thinketh,* is also a must read (www.asamanthinketh.net).[13] The practical application of AI is to catch yourself when you are complaining or being negative and consciously (out loud) ask yourself, "What is *right* or *good* about this situation or experience?"

Accepting and experiencing the prosperity of our inheritance is more than just seeing the glass as half full instead of half empty. The abundant promise allows us to see and expect a full glass, overflowing!

Think about It! When did you last blow something out of proportion? Have you worried about something that is out of your control? Do you know that worry is like a rocking chair? It will give you something to do, but it won't get you anywhere. All worries are reruns that you cannot change.

WE ARE HEDONISTS

All humans by nature avoid pain and seek pleasure, which is part of hedonism. Whether the pain is physical, emotional, spiritual, or a combination of all, we have two basic behavioral choices to alleviate the pain: constructive or destructive.[15, 16]

Destructive behaviors tend to be easier than constructive behaviors, and they are part of the natural bent of the human condition that started in the garden of Eden. Destructive behavior began with the sin of eating from the fruit of the tree of good and evil and has continued ever since. Drugs, alcohol, pornography, and a host of other destructive behaviors are engaged in every day to drown out the pain. The problem with these destructive behaviors is based on the fact that they cause more destruction and pain, thus reinforcing the cycle of depravity.

Selfish hedonistic thinking is part of the depravity wound. The depravity wound is the result of man's choice to sin. Shame, guilt, and lying were the first three hedonistic reactions by Adam and Eve once caught in sin. Obviously, these destructive hedonistic reactions have expanded in the few thousand years since then.

We know that all human spends around 95 percent of the time during waking hours thinking about themselves. However, if we make a conscious choice to spend 1 percent less thinking about ourselves and transferring that energy into thinking about others, we not only enhance the blessings of abundance in our own lives, but also in the lives of those around us.

Selfish hedonism is also related to thinking small (*I Thought versus My Thoughts*). It almost always results in poor conflict resolution as well (e.g., avoidance, control, or compromise). Ideally, we want all conflict resolution to result in synergy. Synergy is a win-win method based on identifying the personal interests or expectations behind each person's position. Synergy centers around good two-way communication getting both parties on the same page. The extra involvement by both parties will result in more effective or alternative solutions in which both parties feel like they have won without compromise.

Think about the last time you had an argument with someone. The natural selfish goal of every argument is to win, which implies the other person loses. However, synergy allows both individuals to win and not feel shorted. This is only possible if we think about ourselves 94 percent of the time and not 95 percent of the time. When we do, the abundance blessings of synergy occur. Choose constructive behavioral choices!

Think about It! Are you making easy choices or difficult ones? Choosing an easy path or a righteous path? What pain needs to be numbed in your life? How did you numb that pain? How much do you think about yourself? Others? Is there something you need to change?

RECAP

Think about It! At this point, you will be thinking one of the following:

1. Yes, I have experienced prosperity from my inheritance. But there is always room for more blessings, as I have many dreams and prayers still waiting to come true.

2. I don't know what they are talking about. My life looks nothing like a blessed, abundant life. This promise of inheritance cannot be true.

If you identify with #1, you will want to know when and where the rest of your inheritance blessings are. Have they been stolen by the Enemy? Have you limited them through selfish and limited thinking?

If the answers were "no" and "no," read on. There are three conditions to the blessings that require action/obedience.

If you identify with #2, you have probably never been upgraded for free to first class. In fact, you may very well be living in a van down by the river. Before you accept this reality and close the book, please ask yourself, "Am I entitled to the inheritance of prosperity?" Are you sure?

Remember that only those who are in the Book of Life are entitled to receive the inheritance. If you believe and accept Jesus is the Son of God as your Lord and Savior, repent of your sins, and acknowledge Him before others (confess with your mouth), you are in the book.

Great. When is the faucet of abundance going to start flowing?

Like a worldly inheritance, you have to ask for it to receive it. Even if you don't exactly know what to ask for, remember that we have a Helper (the Holy Spirit) who intercedes for us. A simple prayer is all that it takes to claim the inheritance of prosperity.

> God, I know you and you know me through Christ my Savior. You are my heavenly Father and I am confidently trusting that you want to bless me. I therefore claim

my inheritance of prosperity and accept the abundant
blessings you have for me in the name of Jesus. Amen.

Of course, humans are not patient creatures by any stretch of the
imagination, and that is part of our DNA wiring. So when will the faucet
of abundance start flowing?

There are three conditions directly related to receiving your
inheritance:

1. **There is an appointed time and place.**

2. **You must use the gifts and talents given to you.**

3. **Your actions and the blessings must glorify God.**

We will be expanding on these three conditions so you can be
blessed abundantly through your inheritance gift from your heavenly
Father. We are anointed to prosper! Remember this is a promise that
endureth to all generations.

REMEMBER ...

Recognizing and avoiding limitations (e.g., thinking small, speaking
negative *have to* self-talk, being not willing to change for growth,
focusing on the negative or on the past and making it larger than it is,
and thinking selfishly) to the inheritance of abundant and joyful life
here on earth is key to experiencing it!

PART 2

At an Appointed Time and Place!

And let us not lose heart and grow weary and faint in acting nobly and doing right, for in due time and at the appointed season we shall reap, if we do not loosen and relax our courage and faint.

Galatians 6:9

CHAPTER 4

God Sometimes Says, "No" or "Not Yet"

> Jeremiah 29:11: "For I know the plans I have for you,"
> declares the LORD, "plans to prosper you and not to harm
> you, plans to give you hope and a future."

KEY IN ON THE WORD *plans*. The word is plural (more than one). How many plans? Two, twenty, two hundred, two thousand? The answer is, "As many as are needed." We have free will and don't always make the best decisions in life. Hence, there are many plans to "prosper" you!

Prosper Yes, we are anointed to prosper. That is our inheritance gift for being children of God. And yes, sometimes God says, "No" or "Not yet."

God cannot and will not answer every prayer with a yes. Ever see the movie *Bruce Almighty*? Actor Jim Carrey gets to play the role of God. Upon receiving the world's prayers via e-mails that numbered in the billions, Bruce thought he'd answer *yes to all*. The results are hilarious but catastrophic chaos! Everyone was a lottery winner. However, the winnings were not seven million dollars but seven dollars, since so many prayed to win.

AT AN APPOINTED TIME/PLACE

Galatians 6:9: "And let us not lose heart and grow weary and faint in acting nobly and doing right, for in due time and at the appointed season we shall reap, if we do not loosen and relax our courage and faint."

Focus on the word *appointed* in the Galatians Scripture. The word simply means "when and where it is right." We reap the rewards (i.e., abundant life) at the appointed season.

The word *disappointment* is commonly used by all of us. *I am disappointed I did not get the promotion at work. I am disappointed that my kids did not call on Father's Day.*

The disappointment that results when our prayers are not answered is real. We have felt it, and you probably have too.

When we feel disappointed, the right thing to do is to understand that it simply means it is *not our appointed time or place* for that prayer to be answered. That is after all the definition of *disappointment*. Assuming, of course, we are not limiting God or ourselves. (Go back and read chapter 3.)

It is also vitally important to understand that everything has an appointed time and place.[17, 18, 19] This also takes the awareness and the ability to have confident trust (faith) that God has your best interests at heart. We often hear people praying for a promotion, a baby, or other tangible things and become disappointed, frustrated, and even angry because it is not their appointed time and place to receive that prayer. Or they received the answer to their prayer and missed it because it came in a different way or form. (Remember *I thought versus My thoughts.*)

However, if we look at this word in context to the abundant life God promises us, it simply means it was not our appointed time for this to happen. Perhaps it will happen in a day, week, month, year, or decade from now. Perhaps it will never happen and that is simply God's will for a better plan and outcome.

Be patient. In the parable of the fig tree (Luke 13:6–9), Jesus instructs us to be patient waiting for fruit (four years). Even then, our prayer may not be answered. Be mindful that unbelief may be interfering.

Mark 9:23–24 "Everything is possible for him who believes. Immediately the boy's father exclaimed, 'I do believe; help me overcome my unbelief!'"

We all have some unbelief from time to time. Belief fluctuates like faith. It rises and falls like a hot air balloon. Are we praying to God to overcome our unbelief? Maybe we should.

God also knows there are some things we cannot simply handle at different times in our lives. There are also four distinct seasons of a person's life to be aware of:

1. Spring (identity). Who are we?

2. Summer (learning and growing). Who are we becoming?

3. Fall (influence). Who are we mentoring and teaching?

4. Winter (sage). What and who are we entrusting the future to?

Think about It! Is it the appointed time and place to hear God's yes? What do I need to change while I wait? Do I have unbelief?

ALL THINGS ... GOOD AND BAD

God sees everything from a different perspective than we do. Not all things (good and bad alike) may make sense to us at the time because we do not have the advantage of His perspective.

Sometimes, the blessing takes moments to manifest. Other times, it takes decades. Remember all things ultimately work for good. (Romans 8:28: "All things work together for good to those who love God.") Yes, even the bad ones.

Even the worst ones! Just ask Dr. Viktor Frankl, Holocaust survivor, author, and psychologist.[13] He wrote the book people need to read if they simply cannot find an answer to this question: why would a good God allow that to happen? *Man's Search for Meaning* is the way to unlock the mysteries of why there is so much pain at times in one's life.

Frankl's basis for seeking understanding is referred to as *logotherapy*. Frankl contends that there is a purpose for every hardship or setback and that the mark of success (unlocking the faucet of abundance blessings) is the ability to find it, embrace it, and move forward. Frankl's *ah-ha* moment occurred many years after he was released from a Nazi concentration camp, having endured unthinkable hardships and watching most of his loved ones tortured and murdered. Years later, he was able to see a bigger picture emerging from a worldview. The secret to Frankl's success is grounded in the fact that only God can answer why.

In the meantime, we can understand *to what ends* a tragedy or suffering has occurred by applying logotherapy. This understanding throws a positive twist on suffering by looking at what good has come from the pain. Of course, time often helps us see *to what ends* more clearly, just like bifocals help us read the newspaper without holding it at arm's length.

However, some sufferings do not ever appear to be answered or understood by logotherapy. So how do we come to grips with these seemingly meaningless tragedies? Is God a sadist? Or does God just not care?

These former questions were asked by nearly every one of the millions of Jews that were systematically exterminated in World War II. The actual reason *why* this was allowed to happen is only known unto Him. Could God have prevented the Holocaust?

Of course! Remember, God simply spoke the heavens and earth into existence. So why did this happen? Was it simply so we could see and appreciate life? To appreciate the American dream? We do not know. How then could the Holocaust be God's mercy in disguise? This can only be evaluated using logotherapy and seeing *to what ends* this tragedy occurred.

MERCY IN DISGUISE

Several merciful things happened because of the Holocaust. Among them are human rights movements (i.e., equality for all races and creeds), religious tolerance, intolerance for genocide, expansion of democracy, expansion of Christianity, and the list goes on and on. God has the utmost respect for free will, even at the hands of an evil man. In any event, the *to what ends* understanding of bad things inevitably revolves around the reality that it is often God's mercy in disguise only revealed at the appointed time and place.[20, 21, 22]

Consider God's mercy surrounding the disease smallpox. This once deadly disease took easily the number of lives that the Holocaust did. So why didn't God snuff out this disease like a candle flame? Only He knows. However, Dr. Jonas Salk, a curious creature indeed, discovered a cure. A vaccine that saved millions of lives. A catalyst for the discovery of hundreds of other vaccines developed for the likes of malaria, influenza, chicken pox, diphtheria, polio, and tetanus, just to name a few. Hundreds of millions of lives have been saved from Dr. Salk's curiosity and search for answers. Those lives were saved by the mercy and grace of God working through Dr. Salk and others like him.

Another agonizing *bad thing* that needs the perspective of mercy in disguise involves the unexpected death of a child. Parents are simply not supposed to outlive their children. How could God allow this to happen? And how could this be mercy in disguise? We can only speculate, based on faith, *to what ends* this occurs since God is the only one who can answer why. A perspective of *to what ends* understanding was shared with us by a good friend, Alan, who had lost his seventeen-year-old daughter in a car accident.

Alan simply stated that the emptiness never goes away. He went on to say that the emptiness can be filled, at least in part, by God and by other people's memories of his daughter. Alan cherishes stories told by friends and family about his daughter because it is the only way he can add to his own memories and fill in those blocks of time when he was not experiencing her life. School, sports, and church activities have all helped to partially fill the chasm of emptiness left in the absence of Alan's daughter.

Alan also shared with me that perhaps God was saving his child from a worse fate than death that only He could know about. Maybe God saw an obstacle in that child's path that they could not overcome. Perhaps God spared her from a deadly and painful disease. We do not know why, and it does not make it any easier to guess.

However, we can see to what ends, as in the case of a child's senseless death resulted in a worldwide crusade. MADD—Mothers Against Drunk Driving—has saved countless innocent lives through education and prevention efforts. This is truly a living testament to what ends a seemingly senseless tragedy occurred.

Another wonderful story about God's mercy in disguise is told in the following story about two traveling angels.

> Two traveling angels stopped to spend the night in the home of a wealthy family. The family was rude and refused to let the angels stay in the mansion's guest room. Instead, the angels were given a small space in the cold basement. As they made their bed on the hard floor, the older angel saw a hole in the wall and repaired it. When the younger angel asked why, the older angel replied, "Things aren't always what they seem."

> The next night, the pair came to rest at the house of a very poor, but very hospitable, farmer and his wife. After sharing what little food they had, the couple let the angels sleep in their bed where they could have a good night's rest. When the sun came up the next morning, the angels found the farmer and his wife in tears. Their only cow, whose milk had been their sole income, lay dead in the field. The younger angel was infuriated and

asked the older angel, "How could you have let this happen? The first man had everything, yet you helped him. The second family had little but was willing to share everything, and you let their only cow die."

"Things aren't always what they seem," the older angel replied. "When we stayed in the basement of the mansion, I noticed there was gold stored in that hole in the wall. Since the owner was so obsessed with greed and unwilling to share his good fortune, I sealed the wall so he wouldn't find it. Then last night as we slept in the farmer's bed, the angel of death came for his wife. I gave him the cow instead. Things aren't always what they seem."

Things truly are not always what they seem to be. This is a particularly important perspective to remember. Even in this story, knowing to what ends a particular suffering occurred could be God's mercy in disguise, which may not come for a long time. We may not be able to immediately see the purpose. And time itself may not fully help heal the pain or help us to see the good of God's mercy.

Think about It! Have you experienced a painful moment? Have you tried to look at it from a different perspective? From a "to what ends" perspective? From a "mercy in disguise" perspective? Would that help you get up and move forward?

ALL THINGS ARE TIME LIMITED

There is a saying that goes, "The difficult takes time. The impossible just takes a little longer." Good and bad alike, nothing lasts forever, at least while we are on this blue and green planet. And if you woke up this morning on this side of the grass, you still have a purpose and God wants you to live it out.[23, 24] Sometimes, that is easier said than done. But just remember the turtle.

TURTLING TECHNIQUE

Turtling is a technique of turning yourself right side up after being knocked on your back. It is the God-given drive inside of people that keeps them going and moving ahead. It is persevering even in the worst situation, knowing that all things work for good at an appointed time and place. Dr. Robert Schuller wrote *Possibility Thinkers Creed* related to perseverance.[25]

> When faced with a mountain I will NOT quit! I will keep on striving until I climb over, find a pass through, tunnel underneath, or simply stay and turn the mountain into a stepping stone to something bigger and better.

> ....
> Mark 11:23: "I tell you the truth, if anyone says to this mountain, 'Go, throw yourself into the sea,' and does not doubt in his heart but believes that what he says will happen, it will be done for him."
> ....

Joel Osteen often cites this Scripture with emphasis that we need to *speak to* our mountains (money problems, sickness, anger, addictions, stress, etc.).[11] This is distinctly different from *speaking about* our mountains. Speaking to the mountain and declaring it has no authority over us is part of our inheritance that will remove the mountain and turn on the blessings of abundance at an appointed time and place. While we may never know *why* a mountain is in our way, we have the authority and power to overcome it at our appointed time and place and see the possibilities of *to what ends*. Yes, you can do all things through Christ!

Move those mountains with turtling perseverance, knowing that all things are time limited and *to what ends* these mountains exist will ultimately be transformed to good. And pray for wisdom while you wait.

Think about It! How are you speaking to your mountains? Are you speaking negative self-talk? ("I'll never be able to overcome this. This mountain has always been a problem for me.") Remove the words *never* and *always* from your negative vocabulary in order to experience abundance in our appointed time and place.

PRAY FOR WISDOM

While we are speaking to our mountains to move, it is also recommended that we pray for wisdom while we wait for our appointed time and place.[26] We have all felt disappointed from time to time. Even Solomon, the wisest king ever.

King Solomon, son of King David (the man after God's own heart), asked God only for one thing before taking the throne. He asked for wisdom. Not gold, silver, or riches … Simply wisdom.

What is wisdom?

Wisdom equals knowledge applied with love.

1 Kings 3:19–24 described King Solomon as the wisest man who ever lived. Interestingly enough, Solomon had nearly two thousand wives and one thousand concubines during his life as king. Hardly what many of us would consider wise, and yet that helps put our lives in perspective with respect to wisdom and its application.

Think about a bad decision you made in the past. Did you balance the decision with objective knowledge and subjective love? Probably not.

Remember that change is necessary for growth, and that is why many of us get those nagging feelings to change jobs, move, or stick it out. Search and pray for wisdom in the decision-making process (before you make that decision). Look for the crux move.

The Crux Move

To most people, a cliff looks like a big chunk of rock better appreciated on relatively flat ground or from the comforts of their car. But those who choose to follow the rock climber's credo "Go climb a rock … Why? … Because it is there" see cracks, indentations, and little ledges that unfold into a roadmap to the top.

Along most routes, there is typically one maneuver far more difficult than all the others. Unusual obstacles make it the toughest spot on the climb. It doesn't matter how far you have come or how easy the climb has been. When you get to this one point, you have three choices:

1. Back down and go home.

2. Stay for a while and hang on as long as you can.

3. Just go for it. Take a calculated risk. Push ahead and make the move, finishing the route to the top.

This is what is referred to as the "crux move," and it can challenge your mind as much as it does your strength. Often the risk is unprecedented. Crux moves are scary and uncomfortable. They can be stressful too. To make matters worse, people are often watching. If you choose to make the move and fall, you face certain embarrassment and, for most rock climbers, serious injury.

However, the fact of the matter is that any mistake we make is typically only known to a select few persons. The other 5.3 billion people on the planet do not have a clue about your past mistakes. This is precisely the reason why you should have the courage to implement crux moves and keep climbing. After all, you will never reach the top unless you take a chance. Preferably a chance that has a decision made with wisdom application (knowledge + love).

Confident trust (faith) that you are being guided to identify and overcome that difficult path will lead you to the blessings of abundance. This is the key to successfully navigating the crux move.

Dr. Jo and I were hiking one day to a place in the path that led to Old Baldy Mountain (the rock picture you saw earlier). The view from the top is unobstructed beauty for miles around in all directions. It is peaceful, quiet, serene, and a blessing to see God's handiwork. But when you are a generous five foot, five and not fond of heights, it takes a lot of *encouragement* to convince you that the forty-foot vertical climb is worth the reward and it is possible if you can locate the crux move.

Fortunately, Dr. Jo allowed me to physically push her up with step-by-step instructions where to place her hands and feet. Success! The view was worth the effort and only realized by taking a calculated risk in confident trust. This is a good example of how God wants us to experience blessings of abundance at different times and places in our lives too. First, we need to be trusting that the reward is worth the effort and risk. Second, we need to follow instructions. Third, we need to appreciate the experience and the reward!

Think about It! What was the last difficult decision you had to make? Did you make it with wisdom (knowledge and love)? What were the results? Would you do it differently if you had to do it over again?

RECAP

Think about It! Have your plans been sidelined by a mountain? What have you done to remove that mountain? How can you transform your mountain problem into a stepping-stone?

_____

_____

_____

_____

REMEMBER ...

God promises us that all things work for our good at the appointed time and place. We do not have the capability to understand *why* bad things happen to God's children, but we can understand *to what ends* these bad things can be transformed to good. All things are time limited and have an appointed time and place. (Acts 17:26: "From one man he made all the nations, that they should inhabit the whole earth; and he marked out their appointed times in history and the boundaries of their lands.")

Pray for wisdom, identify the crux move, and keep persevering toward your abundant future!

CHAPTER 5

Growth Occurs in the Valley

Psalm 23:4: "Even though I walk through the darkest valley, I will fear no evil, for you are with me; your rod and your staff, they comfort me."

*O*N THE PREVIOUS CHAPTER, WE referred to *bad things* as mountains that keep us from experiencing our inheritance gift of joyful abundance in the here and now. A transformative way to now view mountains is from the perspective they provide when we are standing on top of one.

It is safe to assume that most of us would like more mountaintop viewpoints and experiences than trudging through the valley viewpoints and experiences. We equate success, joy, and abundance with the mountaintop experiences. Failure, pain, and suffering are therefore attributed with the valley experiences.

However, realize that nothing grows on top of a mountain. It is simply rock, snow, and ice. In the valley, everything grows! Sunlight (God), amid the shadows in the valley, is present, which allows for growth. Therefore, the difficulty associated with maneuvering through that growth allows us the opportunity to need Him more than we do sitting on the mountain. Hence, *suffering* (growth that occurs in the valley) is actually beneficial and necessary.[25, 27, 28]

THE PURPOSE OF SUFFERING

Life on this planet of blues and greens is most often lived between two extremes. This is our life's journey. It is painful at times, pleasant at others, and always interesting. Suffering is all around us to differing degrees. The images of the 9–11–01 terrorist attacks on New York and Washington, DC, are firmly etched in our American minds. Yet it is easy to become emotionally insulated, numb, and even pessimistic about those in pain all around us. At least, that is, until the suffering becomes purposeful and personal.

Without suffering, we simply float through life's ocean and never fully appreciate the awesome splendor and beauty.

Consider the following example. What would air-conditioning feel like if the temperature were always between 60 and 80 degrees Fahrenheit? Air-conditioning might feel mediocre or okay on an 80-degree day. However, when it is 120 degrees in Arizona, air-conditioning feels awesome. It is totally refreshing and enthusiastically appreciated.

Consider another common example of headaches. Most of us would consider a run-of-the-mill headache as a minor suffering. Painful? Yes. But how much relief is felt when the pain is gone? A lot! To be free of pain feels great. Yet days later, we already begin to take for granted the absence of *brain pain*.

The picture that is beginning to emerge is this. We cannot truly experience the fullness of one emotion, (i.e., pleasure and calm waters) without an experience of the other (i.e., pain and rough seas). Therefore, living a life free of painful experiences becomes mediocre and boring. Lukewarm. We remain blind to the awesomeness of life's ocean. Yet many will argue that we would rather live in mediocrity—the middle ground—where life's pendulum swings slowly from *pretty good* to *not too bad* and forego the experiences of pain and suffering. Especially those of us who have experienced a suffering from the Top 10 Hall of Pain.

1. Death of a loved one (spouse, child, parent, etc.)

2. Disaster, terrorism (9–11–01 or Oklahoma City), etc.

3. War, torture (World Wars I and II, Vietnam), etc.

4. Imprisonment (jail, prison, or slavery)

5. Natural disaster (tornado, hurricane, earthquake, fire, etc.)

6. Unemployment, financial loss, bankruptcy, etc.

7. Health problems (cancer, trauma, paralysis, etc.)

8. Divorce (adultery, scattered families, etc.)

9. Addictions (alcohol, drugs, etc.)

10. Abuse (physical, emotional, or sexual)

As we look at these Hall of Pain sufferings, Arizona heat and headaches do not sound so bad. Hall of Pain sufferings are a 10 on the Richter scale. They rock us to our core. They cause us to see the massiveness of hurricane waves that cause us to give up the fight. They cause us to want to let go of our life raft and drown in the seas of self-pity, worry, and fear. It becomes easy to think nothing good can come of these tragedies.

Pain is real. Pain is personal. Pain is traumatic. It does not matter where we rank our present suffering, it simply hurts. It does not make us feel better to know that it could be worse. Because it could be better—a lot better!

So take heart that all suffer on this earth! And those who do have the opportunity for growth and blessings.

> Romans 5:3–4: "We also glory in our sufferings, because we know that suffering produces perseverance; perseverance, character; and character, hope."

Also, note that many *great* people were born out of Hall of Pain sufferings. They learned to see and appreciate life more fully from their sufferings. They learned to experience the abundant life promise because they were pushed to life's extreme edges of pain and suffering.

GREATNESS MAY RESULT

> 1 Peter 1:6–7: In all this you greatly rejoice, though now for a little while you may have had to suffer grief in all kinds of trials. These have come so that the proven genuineness of your faith—of greater worth than gold, which perishes even though refined by fire—may result in praise, glory, and honor when Jesus Christ is revealed.

Each suffering event provides us with an opportunity to grow in our faith. Faith is simply *confident trust* that all things really do work together for our good. The more trials, the greater the faith, the greater the blessings, the greater the person.[29]

In 1962, Victor and Mildred Goertzel published a study entitled "Cradles of Eminence." The authors studied the backgrounds of great leaders of the world and found a common thread. Tragedy, difficulty, and suffering befell all of these people in order to become the *great* people and leaders that God wanted them to be.

According to the Goertzel's research, painful failures and sufferings were common among the likes of Winston Churchill, Abraham Lincoln, George Washington, and many other famous leaders.

Pride and arrogance did not create these people's greatness. Rather, the common thread among these great leaders that we have noticed is the *humility* that resulted from their suffering. Humility is simply modesty of one's own importance (putting others' value equal or greater than your own), and being comfortable with who you are (good, bad, and ugly). Humility is what binds these great people together, as well as many others not mentioned in Goertzel's study.

Consider Richard Bach. Bach was a pilot who became editor of an aviation magazine that went bankrupt. His life was riddled with repeated failures that humbled him. During those humble sufferings, he wrote *Jonathan Livingston Seagull*. Eighteen publishers initially rejected it before it was finally published. It sold seven million copies and made Bach a well-known and respected author.

Also, consider a figure in Goertzel's original research, Abraham Lincoln. Raised in Illinois, Lincoln became a lawyer and was called to politics. Numerous failures marked his early campaigns for governor, congressman, and senator twice. Yet with the help of God, he found the courage to run and become elected as our sixteenth president of the United States. The rest is history.

Out of the ashes of pain and suffering, humility allows for true greatness among the most influential people of history. Yet it is easy for us to rationalize or diminish these people's pain and suffering on paper. It is easy to see the wonderful end results without experiencing their pain. And it is equally easy to say, "Nobody knows the trouble I've seen," when we ourselves experience the Hall of Pain. What then?

Think about It! Are you blinded by the pain of suffering? Do you know that you have "great" company? Can you see the "to what ends" purpose for suffering in context with growth/outcomes/benefits?

IMAGINE THE POSSIBLE

James Allen[9] author of *As A Man Thinketh* stated, "Until thought is linked with purpose (goals/mission) there is no intelligent accomplishment."

Creating a vision of what is possible as a result of walking through the valley of suffering is incredibly important in order to attain and experience the benefits from that suffering described in Romans 5. Envisioning the possible is related to self-efficacy.

Self-efficacy is simply your ability to make things happen that you want to happen. Self-efficacy increases by affirming who we are (a child of the Most High God, entitled to an inheritance of joyful abundance).

An affirmation is a vow, promise, or contract with self. It is always first-person present, and behavior changes on a subconscious level. Our subconscious is a servomechanism. It does what we tell it. If we tell it, "This is easy," "This is great," "I want to," or "I choose to" it will be. However, we only need to affirm, "I hate liver," once, and it is ingrained in our subconscious forever. So affirm what you want, otherwise it's just good intentions and your life will look pretty much like it is today.

Affirm what we want our lives to be and set dreams you never thought possible; allow yourself to grow into them. We draw to ourselves the relationships, jobs, income, and successes we feel worthy of receiving. If we do not fee worthy of success, we will push it away and rationalize it. It is essential for us to believe we are worthy of an abundant life before we can attain it!

One human emotion that limits our vision of possibility and abundance is fear.

OVERCOME FEAR

How do the best of the best overcome fear? Fear of failure? Fear of rejection?

Quite simply, they have the ability in their mind to see what it is going to look like once they are through it. They hold the vision of success in their mind at all times. They then control fear. It is not to say that successful people are not afraid. They feel fear, but they do not stay afraid.[30, 31] They are willing to take risks, willing to make changes, and willing to fail to win. Michael Jordan once said, "I've taken over 40,000 shots in my career and missed nearly 20 percent of them, but I am still a winner with six championship rings and so are my teammates." What would have happened if Jordan let his fear of missing a shot interfere with intended actions?

Some of our favorite movies based on true stories were those where the underdog wins, where there is victory in seemingly certain defeat (*Rocky, Rudy, Soul Surfer, Field of Dreams*, and many, many others). There is triumph that rises from the ashes like in the movie *We Are Marshall*. Coach Lengyel overcame the fear of not being able to successfully coach a team after such a major tragedy. The actions of Coach Lengyel ultimately led to the healing of the town, the school, and the team!

Another example of succeeding in the face of fear can be easily referenced from a world-champion rodeo clown. His job is to entertain the audience and provide for the safety of the rodeo participants by putting his life on the line. At any moment, the rodeo clown could be easily maimed or killed by a three-thousand-pound bull. But when asked how they control the fear that they must feel in these life-and-death situations, their universal answer is, "We see past the performance to a picture of successfully sitting down with our family and eating dinner after the rodeo." As long as they hold this picture of success in their mind, fear will not overcome them and cause them to freeze up.

Those who are afraid and see only fear do nothing. Those who are afraid but visualize success do everything! James Allen stated, "He who has conquered doubt and fear has conquered failure."

As professors, we challenge students every day to face their fears of failure and their fears of mistakes by exchanging them for endless opportunities to grow and learn. Dr. Jo coaches and counsels clients daily to face their fears and develop higher understanding of their biological, psychological, social, and spiritual potential. As a physical therapist, Dr. Eric challenges patients to overcome their fears of pain and exchange it for function and healing. What we can do in the absence of fear is limitless!

....

1 John 4:18: "Perfect love drives out fear."

....

Christ, therefore, allows us to overcome fear.

Think about It! What are you most afraid of? Should you be afraid? What are the consequences of fear? How is fear limiting your inheritance of abundance?

SELF-IMAGE

Another factor that limits our vision of possibility and abundance is based on our self-image.

....

Genesis 1:27: "So God created man in His own image, in the image of God he created them; male and female He created them."

....

Our self-image is quite simply the way we see ourselves in honest and truthful appraisal. It is our subconscious opinion of ourselves and what we have come to expect from ourselves. Much of how we *feel* about ourselves comes from our past experiences and what others have said to us or about us. This input can result in positive or negative self-image.

Do you see yourself as *motivated* and *eager to learn,* or do you see yourself as *lazy* and *underachieving*? Your actions will convey your true self-image. It cannot be faked.[32]

CHOOSE WHO-SAIDS CAREFULLY

Part of our self-image comes from affirmations or statements from *who-saids* that we believe have the authority or power to do so.[5] Who-saids are people in our lives that we grant authority or power to. For example, many of us consider our spouses, parents, teachers, clergy, and close friends as who-saids. That is to say, we believe what they tell us about ourselves. If they tell us we are smart and funny, we incorporate that into our self-image and behave that way. However, if they tell us we are dumb and incorrigible, we also incorporate that into our self-image and behave accordingly.

In the movie *The Wizard of Oz*, the scarecrow, lion, and tin man were looking for brains, courage, and a heart, because they were told these were lacking in their self-image. All three were looking for a who-said to affirm or grant them something they already had, but needed permission or sanction to use it. The wizard, of course, was a fraud, but the characters believed what he said because they viewed him as an authoritative who-said. So be careful about who you consider a who-said, and be doubly careful about incorporating what they say into your self-image.

For example, there is a popular true story about a zipper manufacturer that was going out of business in the 1920s unless sales picked up. One day, the owner challenged the employees to come up with a solution to selling more zippers. Thinking of ways to use zippers, one of the employees had an illumination (ah-ha) experience. So he rushed into the boss and said, "I've got it, why don't we put zippers in men's pants. It's never been done before. We've always used buttons. And you know how many pairs of men's pants there are." The boss replied, "That's the stupidest idea I've ever heard. Do you know the lawsuits we could have if someone zipped themselves up in the zipper." Initially crushed and dejected by the boss' comments, this person recognized that his boss was not a who-said. The man lost his job as the company went out of business. However, the man's wife encouraged him to follow his dreams, knowing it was a great opportunity. She was a who-said in his life, and this man went on to manufacturer his own zippers and sell them in men's pants around the world, securing for himself a fortune of his own. Yes, he is the founder of YKK, the largest zipper manufacturer in the world today. It produces more than two thousand miles of zippers each day. His name is Yoshida Kogyo Kabushikikaisha.

Who-saids have Pygmalion transformation power. In Greek mythology, you will find a character called Pygmalion. He was a sculptor, and a very good one at that. One day, he completed a sculpture of a woman with such likeness and beauty that he fell in love with her. Not the kind of love you might have for a car. We mean real love like he wanted to marry her. He was a little different. As the story goes, the goddess of love appeased his wish and shot an arrow into the heart of the sculpture, transforming her into a real person whom Pygmalion married. They lived happily ever after.

The classic movie *My Fair Lady* was based on Pygmalion transformation. In this movie, Professor Higgins thought he was such a good Pygmalion that he could take the lowliest flower girl off the streets of London (Eliza Doolittle) and class her all up and pass her off as royalty. Higgins succeeded as a who-said because Eliza saw him as one.

Years ago, Olympic champion Charley Paddock was speaking to the young men at East Tech High School in Cleveland, Ohio. "If you think you can, you can!" he challenged the youths. "If you believe a thing strongly enough, it can come to pass in your life!" Afterward, a spindly-legged boy said to Mr. Paddock, "Gee, sir, I'd give anything if I could be an Olympic champion just like you!" It was that lad's moment of inspiration. His life changed. In 1936, that young man went to Berlin, Germany, to compete in the Olympics. He came home with four gold medals! His name was Jesse Owens. Paddock succeeded as a who-said because Owens saw him as one.

A researcher in California tested the power of who-saids by providing teachers of first graders with fake data showing *spurters* (kids that had it but weren't using it). He tested the kids and generated fake data to provide to the teachers. Those he identified as spurters rose to the top of the class and stayed there. The others were treated like it was about all the better they could do, and they did subpar work. Another example of who-said transformational power of one's self-image.

Believe in yourself. You are also your own Pygmalion who-said.

James Allen said it best: "As a man thinketh, so he is." I believe this also applies: "As a person thinketh another is, so they are."

We see this every day in the counseling office during individual and conjoint sessions. Some have experienced negative who-said input in their childhood from their parents and spouses related to emotional, physical, and sexual abuses. When this is not transformed, it is carried with them into their adult relationships. We also see this in adults who had generally positive childhood who-said input but are now confronted with negative spousal who-said input.

When things are not going well for couples, one spouse might be more blaming of the other. Conversations usually start with, "Because of you, we do not have any money …" "We're in debt up to our eyeballs …"

"We don't have any friends ..." "We never have sex anymore ..." Whether the husband or the wife, who-saids can make a person feel like everything is their fault. The problem is obvious in context with what a who-said is supposed to do: empower, champion, support, and motivate. For who-saids to be positive and effective on another's self-image, they must demonstrate the golden rule: do unto others (and say unto others) as you would have them do unto you.

Dr. Jo also sees this in family therapy where there is an *identified patient*, usually a child. All too often, parents feel that they are wonderful positive who-said parents and all of their children except *the one* (identified patient) are great. They want the identified child *fixed*, and yet many times it is the family system of who-saids interacting with each other that is actually the source of the problem.

Symptoms are easy to recognize, but problems are often not. If you focus on solving symptoms, the problems remain. However, when the problems are recognized, there must be a commitment of agreement to change behavior by all involved in order to solve them and eliminate the resultant symptoms. Those who are willing to change can again become *positive* who-said influences. Those who are not willing to change will continue to be *negative* who-said influences and *chaos* is the universal characteristic in their lives.

Chaos is defined as "complete disorder and confusion." We will talk in more detail about this and how to keep it from limiting our inheritance of joyful abundance in chapter 8.

Joanna is my who-said, and I am hers. We champion each other to be wiser, more courageous, stronger, smarter, and to inspire big dreams. Together, we are able to grow in the valley of suffering in order to emerge better and experience blessings of abundance not possible alone. So be a positive who-said to those around you! You will be blessed just as much, if not more, as they will be.

Think about It! How do you see yourself in the mirror? Who have you been listening to that have shaped your self-image? Were they positive or negative influences? Who are your true who-saids?

RECAP

Think about It! Have you been in the valley of suffering long enough? Is fear limiting your vision for what is possible during this valley experience? How can you apply changes to your self-image in order to exit the valley of suffering better than before you went in?

_____

_____

_____

_____

REMEMBER ...

The greater the suffering, the greater the opportunity for greatness to emerge! Fear is a *false expectation appearing real* and therefore has no power to prevent your inheritance of abundance. Your self-image is based on the Creator, the ultimate *Who-said.*

CHAPTER 6

Out of Egypt

*O*N THE OLD TESTAMENT, ONE of the most widely known stories is about Moses leading God's people out of Egypt to the Promised Land. While the miracles abound in this story, something prevented the people from entering the Promised Land. Moses and his people wandered the desert for forty years. Why?

Moses committed murder in Exodus 2:11–14, but that was not the reason God did not allow him to enter the Promised Land. The only reference to why Moses was not allowed to enter Canaan is alluded to in Numbers 20:8–13 when Moses *struck* the rock with his staff out of anger to produce water instead of following God's instructions to *speak* to the rock.

Now this seems like quite a severe punishment for a seemingly *technical sin*. Especially given all of the great things Moses had done in the name of God the Father. However, Moses did receive what he ultimately wanted: freedom from leading the stubborn Israelites. In fact, God buried Moses Himself and Moses' body was nowhere to be found. Second, God blessed Moses with good health and is described at his death as full of vigor. Third, Moses was needed to complete a picture that God wants all of us to see. Obedience precedes the abundance of blessings.

What is really interesting about the story of Moses is the fact that Moses appeared to be punished by God for an act of disobedience—an act of anger by striking the rock with his staff to produce water for the complaining Israelites instead of speaking to the rock. The punishment seems so much more severe to us than Moses' earlier acts of anger, such as killing the Egyptian or throwing down the Ten Commandments and breaking them. So why did God levy such a severe consequence?

The short answer is that we don't know, because we are not God. But we can explore *to what ends*. God got His point across that obedience precedes blessings. Case in point, Joshua was instructed to be strong and courageous. He trusted and obeyed God's word and was blessed with the abundance of the Promised Land. Those who complained and were afraid never did enter the land of abundance.

I WANT TO GO BACK

While we are waiting for our appointed time and place to experience the inheritance of abundant life, it can become easy to criticize, complain, and want to go back, especially if we are walking through a valley of suffering. The words of Sarah Groves' song "I've Been Painting Pictures of Egypt" ring true.

> I've been painting pictures of Egypt,
> leaving out what it lacked.
> The future looks so hard,
> and I want to go back.

When we succumb to negativity, we paint pictures of Egypt and *look back* much *too long*. We don't see what was lacking in the past. We tend to see things through rose-colored glasses. We forget the pain or what it was really like. We only see valley, jungle, difficulty, and pain in front of us. And we want to go back.

The problem with wishing to go back is that God loves us too much to let us stay the same. We will simply stay longer in the valley of suffering until we can break out of the negativity. Until we can create that vision for what is on the other side of this valley.

The past has a purpose (much like the rear-view mirror of a car). However, if you focus too much on the past (rear-view mirror), you will not be able to move forward (without crashing). The past gives us context to see what was wrong or lacking in our lives with each blessing of abundance. Those obedient actions of patience, perseverance, and intention are then transformed into abundance keys to success!

In 1961, Jerry Richardson faced an important decision. He was a wide receiver for the Baltimore Colts but did not receive a raise that he had requested. He could play at the same pay as last year or do something he always wanted to do: start his own business. Richardson and his family moved back to South Carolina where he bought a hamburger stand. Richardson bought the first Hardee's franchise. His pay was $417 dollars a month. Some would have thought it was time to punt. Tired and frustrated as he was, Richardson refused to give up. He employed the same discipline he had used on the football field to focus on making his restaurant more efficient, his employees the friendliest in town, and his prices affordable. Before long, his business boomed. He was able to purchase the NFL's Carolina Panthers in 1993 and continues to head one of the largest food-service companies in the United States. It has $3.7 billion a year in sales.

It would have been easier for Richardson to go back to his NFL playing career. But we all know that would not last forever. Instead, Richardson sought wise counsel and started envisioning the future of abundance just around the corner of this valley suffering. When patience, perseverance, and intention are applied in obedience, awesome things happen at their appointed time and place.

We have all heard the phrases *you can never go back, you can never go home,* and *the good ole days.* These statements reflect a desire to live in the past, which steals from the present and prevents an intentional future. Therefore, we are encouraged to praise God in all we do at all times, especially in the storms of life. When we do, blessings of abundance occur.

Two very high-profile examples come to mind here. In 2005, Tony Dungy and his wife Lauren lost their eighteen-year-old son to suicide. In 2008, Steven Curtis Chapman (popular Christian song-writer/musician) and his wife Mary Beth lost their five-year-old daughter to a car accident. In both cases, they were quickly giving speeches on TV, radio, and in person to all who would listen. They said that they chose to continue praising God in these storms of tragedy and grow in the valley of the shadow of death until they emerged stronger and better with God and for God. They did it the way God wanted the Israelites to leave Egypt and enter the Promised Land. As most are aware, the careers and influence of Dungy and Chapman continue to increase exponentially.

Think about It! Are you complaining in your valley of suffering? Are you obedient and trusting God's Word? How else are you going to get out of that valley?

PRUNING MAY BE NECESSARY

If you answered *no* and *yes* to the "Think about It" questions, remember the variable of time and place still apply. Dr. Bruce Wilkinson did a great job talking about *pruning* in these valley moments in the book *Secrets of the Vine*.[33]

In the book, Wilkinson speaks of the metaphor between farming grapes and growing faith through valley-suffering experiences. The farmer knows that in order to produce the best grapes, the vines must be pruned. Similarly, our Father knows how to produce the best child by cutting away parts of our lives that interfere with growth. No pruning is an enjoyable experience at the time. But at the harvest, the abundance of fruit and blessings produced are worth the time-limited suffering.

One perspective that is important to delineate related to pruning (loss of something) is to recognize the source. This helps eliminate anger and unforgiveness, which keep us in the valley of suffering longer than needed. To help determine the source of loss, the following steps will help:

1. **Sit Tight** – Don't make any rash decisions. Get the Bible out of the trashcan and *pray until something happens* (PUSH).

2. **Think Logically** – and not emotionally. Satan thrives on emotions of anger guilt, shame, doubt, and depression.

3. **Don't Take It Personally** – Don't assume your pain is punishment for your past sins. Remember God sees the big picture and takes no pleasure in seeing us suffer.

4. **It Don't Make Worse Than It Is** – Don't become fatalistic. It is not the end, unless you give up and make it your end.

5. **Check Your Value System** – Know what is really important, like family and everlasting life.

6. **Listen to Wise Counsel** – Hear what those who love you and God think.

7. **Think Positively** – Don't ever give up. God knows the plans He has for you are good, to give you a future and a hope.

It is easy to want to give up or get mad when we experience a loss, especially when someone else can be blamed. However, a lack of forgiveness results in the inability to see the bigger picture. It keeps us stuck were we are.

If you can still read your Bible, pray, and find some measure of logic in the loss, do not take it personally. Do not make it the be-all-end-all. Keep God and family more important than the circumstances. Actually listen to brothers and sisters in Christ and see something positive (even if it is ridiculous). Then the Source is most likely your heavenly Father pruning something in your life. However, sometimes it is just plain obvious that the source of loss is obviously the Enemy.

WE MAY HAVE BEEN ROBBED

The Enemy has only three goals: to steal, to kill, and to destroy. This can be literal or metaphorical (killing dreams, destroying relationships, stealing faith). He does this by lying to us. If we believe the lies *you're not worthy, you're not good enough,* or *you don't deserve blessings,* it steals our joy, takes away from our faith (confident trust), and limits the blessings we are entitled to inherit and experience.

> Proverbs 6:31: "Yet if he is caught, he must pay sevenfold."

As long as we were not the cause of the loss (i.e., bad decision making), we have a promise of restitution. If we recognize the thief has stolen something from us, one of the best things to do is tally up the loss. This is easiest to do in terms of dollars and cents.

For example, a few years ago we built a home in South Carolina and closed on it with no liens or encumbrances. Two months later, we were served court papers that a mechanics lien was filed on behalf of two subcontractors that the builder had never paid. We did not do anything to deserve this debt and the monetary theft was easy to determine.

Emotionally distraught at first and angry at the builder for his lack of morals and outright theft, we later realized who was at true fault here. This was the Devil stealing our joy in the new home. We then prayed to God based on the Proverbs promise:

Heavenly Father, You know who has stolen from us and we are standing on Your promise to make him pay seven times the amount stolen. Unleash the angels of heaven to turn him upside down and shake out the $42,000 he now owes us here on earth. We trust You will deliver on Your promise.

Then we waited, praised God for what we did have, and He delivered.

We were called to Fernandina Beach, Florida, a few years later in a horribly depressed housing market. But we were obedient and listed the house. The home we had built in South Carolina was one of only two houses to close in the area in the past twenty-four months, and we fully recouped the loss in terms of gain and savings against continued depression of housing prices.

This is a *Go-God-Awesome* blessing when it arrives! One of many we have experienced over the years with continued confidence that many more will come.

Another personal experience involves job losses. Despite stellar performance reviews, we have experienced unexpected job losses as a result of various leadership changes and institutional cutbacks. Instead of getting stuck in the anger of the loss, we recognized the source of the theft and prayed for it to be returned sevenfold, believing it would happen. We kept using our gifts and talents to start a new company offering support services to graduate students and health-care consulting services that continue to receive clients and referrals six years later without one dollar of marketing spent to promote it. We believe the blessings will continue based on God's promise in Proverbs.

Think about It! How angry are you when something is stolen from you? Have you prayed to make the Enemy repay you seven times for the amount he stole? Once you do pray this, are you less angry?

Hopefully your answer to the last "Think about It" question is *yes*. Anger is the natural reaction to loss, which leads to unforgiveness.

Most are familiar with the story of *Moby Dick* by Herman Melville. In the story, Captain Ahab spent years searching out the white whale that had crippled him. His anger led him on this mission of revenge. When Ahab found the whale, he was so filled with rage that he is described this way: "And he piled upon the whale's white hump the sum of all the rage and hate. If his chest had been a canon, he would have shot his heart upon it." Then Ahab realized that his anger nearly cost him and his crew their very lives. He saw there could be victory in his restraint.

VICTORY IN RESTRAINT

The Old Testament story of King David's restraint in not seeking revenge and killing King Saul is widely known and told. In that story, King Saul was very jealous of David and tried to have David killed on at least two occasions. When David had the opportunity for revenge, he stopped short and only cut a piece of King Saul's robe. David's restraint caused King Saul to see the error of his anger. Forgiveness was granted. And forgiveness defeated anger.

Experience forgiveness today starting with yourself. Yes, we must forgive ourselves first for all our mistakes and trespasses. We must also forgive others who have hurt us in order to release us from our own bondage (prison). Again, forgiveness is for our own benefit, and it will release the abundant blessings promised all of us. It is also a mandate in the Lord's Prayer to *forgive others as we have been forgiven.*

TO LOVE IS TO FORGIVE; TO FORGIVE IS TO LOVE

1 Corinthians 13 is known as the love chapter. It states that love does not remember the wrongs of the past. This statement presents a unique catch-22. Love forgives and forgets the wrongs of the past, and forgiveness is a unique expression of love. Without love, we cannot forgive. Without forgiveness, we cannot love. Love and forgiveness are inexorably intertwined by God. We forgive to the degree we love. We love to the degree we forgive.

The ability to love and forgive is impossible if two conditions are not present. First, God must be in our lives. Second, we must be able to separate the action from the person. Hate the sin, but love the sinner. Without both of these conditions, we are locked into the inability to love or forgive keeping us from experiencing the abundant life blessings God promises us. This is an obvious lose-lose outcome that the Enemy would declare victory. The Enemy is not entitled to this victory. We must choose to give it to him. The choice is ours!

Think about It! Do you love others? Have you forgiven them too? Even your enemies? If not, how can you truly love?

RECAP

Think about It! Have you been looking backward more than forward? How can you know where you are heading then? Is anger limiting your ability to forgive and love?

_____

_____

_____

_____

REMEMBER ...

In order to exit Egypt (the suffering/loss valley), we should obey, look forward, forgive, and pray. There is power in prayer and a promise of a sevenfold return on what is stolen from us. Even greater blessings await those whose loss is part of God's pruning process. In both cases, forgiveness replaces anger, resentment, and bitterness and turns on the faucet of abundance in our lives. Then you can feel and hear the peace all around you.

Part 3

When We Use Our Talents and Gifts!

There are different kinds of gifts, but the same Spirit. There are different kinds of service, but the same Lord. There are different kinds of working, but the same God works all of them in all men ... wisdom ... knowledge ... faith ... healing ... miraculous powers ... prophecy ... distinguishing between spirits ... speaking in tongues ... interpretation of tongues.

1 Corinthians 12:4–11

CHAPTER 7

What Is Your IQ?

*I*T IS MOST IMPORTANT TO understand how our talents/gifts are related to the inheritance of a joyful and abundant life. The words *joy* and *gifts* are derived from the same Greek root word, *charis* (khar-ece), which includes the meanings of benefit, favor, graciousness, and pleasure, among others. In short, abundant joy comes when we use our gifts. Therefore, identifying our gifts is a universal first step.

It is interesting to discuss the gifts and talents bestowed on us by our Creator. Many people start with an incorrect proposition that if they do not have *all* of the spiritual gifts, God loves them less. The key verbiage in the first letter to Corinthians, chapter 12, focuses on this: "He distributes them to each one just as He determines." It does not say that He distributes *all* of them. Rather just the ones He determines. Each of us is unique, and our gifting is designed to glorify Him. Therefore, we may have one gift, or all twenty-three of them. Yes, there are twenty-three possible gifts cited throughout the Bible, and all of us have at least one!

TWENTY-THREE POSSIBLE GIFTS

Dr. Mels Carbonell has created a self-administered survey to assess your spiritual gifts profile (www.myuy.com).[34] It is an investment in knowing yourself better and where your natural gifting strengths are. Everyone has at least one ten-scale gift from the following twenty-three options: administration/ruling, craftsmanship, discernment, evangelism, apostleship/pioneering, creative communication, encouraging/exhorting, faith, giving, hospitality, interpretation, leadership, healing, intercession, knowledge, mercy, miracles, prophecy/proclaiming/perceiving, teaching, wisdom, pastor/shepherding, serving/ministry/helping, and tongues. Most of us can identify at least one from the list. Dr. Carbonell has also provided a one-word description of each of the twenty-three gifts that further helps hone in on the ones we most identify with: initiator, handy, listener/perceiver; dynamic, visionary, actor/actress, encourager, optimist, steward, sociable, translator, dreamer, restorer, prayer warrior, divine insights, caring, powerful, bold, in-depth, perceptive, discipler, selfless, and conduit.

FIFTEEN TO SIXTEEN PERSONALITY TYPES

If you have never taken a personality test, it is helpful to know in order to optimize your gifts. Two of the most validated and popular personality tests include the Myers-Briggs and DISC profile tests.[35]

The Myers-Briggs Personality Test reveals sixteen possible combinations (ISTJ, ISFJ, INFJ, INTJ, ISTP, ISFP, INFP, INTP, ESTP, ESFP, ENFP, ENTP, ESTJ, ESFJ, ENFJ, and ENTJ) based on the four dichotomies of personality:

> Extraversion (E) or Introversion (I)
> Sensing (S) or Intuition (N)
> Thinking (T) or Feeling (F)
> Judging (J) or Perception (P)

Similarly, the DISC Personality Profile also reveals fifteen personality patterns (achiever, agent, appraiser, counselor, creative, developer, inspirational, investigator, objective thinker, perfectionist, persuader, practitioner, promoter, result-oriented, specialist) based on four personality characteristics:

Driven (D) (other terms include dominating, directing, determined, demanding)

Influential (I) (other terms include inspiring, inducing, impressing)

Steadfast (S) (other terms include stable, servant, submissive)

Cautious (C) (other terms include competent, compliant, contemplative)

These personality characteristics are then delineated by assertive (A) – passive (P) and task (T) – people (P) dichotomies.

UNLIMITED COMBINATIONS

The combinations of gifts (twenty-three) and personality types (fifteen or sixteen) result in more than twenty trillion possibilities. Yes, we used an online math permutation calculator to determine this, and we are truly glad that God keeps track of this math! In any event, the possibilities support the fact that we are all truly made unique.

Also, think about how unique Jesus was. Remember back to the story of His birth. Shortly after it, King Herod had all of the baby boys in Bethlehem and surrounding area who were two years old and under killed. Of course, the angels guided Joseph, Mary, and Jesus to Egypt during that time. Eventually, they returned to the surrounding town of Nazareth. But think of how unique this child would be to that area.

In a crowd of boys, there would be newborns and six-year-olds, but only one three-year-old (Jesus), since Herod had killed all the others. He would have been a unique teenager and adult too. His twelve disciples most certainly would have been two to three years older or younger than he. Again, during the ministry years, Jesus was a unique man among men for reasons beyond the miracles and teachings! One can assume then that God likes unique people because they stand out and are recognizable. They are intentional.

LIFE IS NOT FUTILE

We all have a *unique* purpose in life.[24] God calls us to love Him and one another. And God gives us special gifts to use for His purposes. Some are given strong arms and legs to build things with. Others may be given extra smartness to think and invent useful things we need. Still others may be given the ability to teach or heal people. We all have special gifts. We all have a special purpose, just as Jesus had a special purpose.

Think about It! What are your gifts/talents? What is your personality profile? How do your gifts/talents and personality work together and make you unique? How are you using your gifts/talents and personality to lead a purpose-driven life?

KNOW THYSELF

The maxim *know thyself* originated with Socrates (Greek philosopher) some four hundred years before Jesus was born. Most, however, do not know the rest of the maxim, which is *know thyself in order to be wise.* Remember wisdom is knowledge applied in love (an action proposition). As we have discussed earlier, we benefit from a forward-looking vision to steer our future intentionally toward blessings and away from curses. When we know ourselves, we can make wiser decisions.[36]

What happens if you cannot identify your ten talents/gifts?

The short answer is that we end up working at jobs because of happenstance and become frustrated, stressed, and too busy to take the time to change jobs or truly recognize what we should be doing. The doldrums of life occur because people do not know what their talents/gifts are, and therefore they do not work in careers where they can use them.

Think about the individual who goes to college and gets a degree in hospitality. They have a mid-management position at a national hotel chain but are so frustrated and stressed with their career that they bring it home to their family, which starts causing problems. When asked why they chose to work in hospitality, the answer would be something like, "My guidance counselor told me I'd always have a job." Then we ask, "Do you know what your gifting is? What you are good at?

What is fun and natural to you?" The initial answer is usually, "No" or "Not really," but in time we find out together that the person's gifting is in a completely different area like healing. Once the true gifting is determined, we can set goals in your life to use them and reap an abundance of blessings in return.

TAKE ACTION

Some have been given more talents and gifts than others. All are different and none should feel inadequate or inferior to another. We are all stars in the sky. Some in the east, some in the west, some large, some small, some bright yellow, some bright white, but we are all stars!

Also, focus on the word *use*. We must do something with our gifts or they are wasted. How good are the best intentions without action? Can dreams become reality without action?

1 Corinthians 3:8: "The one who plants and the one who waters have one purpose, and they will each be rewarded according to their own labor."

We are rewarded for using (giving) our gifts/talents.

RECAP

Think about It! Do you see the connection between experiencing the abundant life and using your gifts/talents according to your personality? What are your gifts/talents? How are you using them? How might you learn more about yourself to work fully in your gifting/talent area to maximize the blessings of abundance in your life?

_____

_____

_____

_____

REMEMBER ...

We are made uniquely indeed! To shine for His glory. Therefore, we should all know our natural skills and talent gifts, our personality, and take action, as we all have a responsibility to use our gifts accordingly. When we do, at our appointed time and place, for the glory of God, the experience of our abundant life promise will occur.

CHAPTER 8

Authentic Man, Authentic Woman

ONE SURE WAY TO SHORTCHANGE our inheritance of abundance is to live outside of the design for man and woman separate, and together. Let's start by asking simple questions.

- » What is a real man?
- » An authentic man?
- » How do you know you are a man?
- » What is a real woman?
- » An authentic woman?
- » How do you know you are a woman?

If you reflected on these questions for any length of time, you probably concluded that these are not such easy questions to concretely answer, and yet they should be. The reality is that our answers are often influenced by modern culture instead of correct design grounded in Genesis.

An article written by Richard Conniff in 2012 explored the basis for why casually disparaging the entire male gender is a national pastime and the only last socially acceptable prejudice. His survey asked men and women to name a few things men do well. The answers were nearly all negative and included things like leaving the toilet seat up or nothing. The conclusion Conniff arrived at is that men are a necessary evil and maybe not all that necessary. So where and how did we get so far off track as a culture not to see value in men?

Boys are more disruptive in school, take more medications for attention deficit disorder than girls, and drop out of high school and college twice as often as girls. Young men are more likely to be aggressive and violent, and they are incarcerated five times more than females. More than 38 percent of men are absent fathers, and the list goes on. Television, movies, music, and other popular media commonly promote the idiocy of men at an alarmingly popular rate, which only propagates the problems. Unfortunately, a majority of men do not fight these negative stereotypes because they are viewed as funny or help justify their own debauchery with the statement, "At least I don't _____ (fill in the blank for a popular TV/movie character's behavior)." Women have their list of shortcomings too, but we want to start with men because that is where God started. He created man first. He also set forth the pillars of authenticity for men and women.

Much of this chapter is based on the four pillars of authentic manhood written by Dr. Robert Lewis and the original Men's Fraternity material.[37] Men and women are encouraged to read both sections in order to know God's plan for each other. Let's start with authentic men.

FOUR PILLARS OF AUTHENTIC MANHOOD AND WOMANHOOD

To answer the questions at the beginning of this chapter, we must go to Genesis to find the answers. There are four principles or tenets that are essential for being (living) as an authentic man or woman:

1. **Accept Christ.**

2. **Reject passivity.**

3. **Accept responsibility.**

4. **Invest eternally.**

We believe that receiving the inheritance of abundant blessings is only possible when men and women live authentically. We also believe that the root of societal problems starts here. It is biblical, and we have experienced it firsthand.

ACCEPT CHRIST.

We know that many accept Jesus as the Son of God at a variety of different ages. This is the foundation for authenticity regardless of age. It is required in order to be anointed to prosper and receive our inheritance of abundant blessings here on earth. However, we want to place in context the discussion of authentic man and woman based on the adult.

First, we will start with a basis that a man/woman is roughly aged eighteen or older. There are physiological reasons for this based on development (physical and mental). For example, the frontal lobe of the brain is not fully developed until at least age twenty-one, and the area responsible for judgment, emotion, and memory. In other words, we don't make wise decisions until our brain physically allows it to happen. Second, we look to Jesus as a model. He did not start formal ministry until He was thirty years of age. Part of this had to do with His appointed time and place. We also know that Jesus was fully man and developed physically as a man. In any event, we are talking about authentic adults (men and women) who have accepted Jesus as their Lord and Savior.

REJECT PASSIVITY AND ACCEPT RESPONSIBILITY.

Passivity and a lack of responsibility are directly related to the fall of man in the garden of Eden. Adam was passive and deferred to Eve's leadership when she presented the fruit to him, sinning against God. Then they tried to hide and make excuses for their actions. (See Genesis

3:12.) Adam was passive (to God, not listening or obeying) and did not accept his responsibility to lead. Eve was passive (to God, not listening or obeying) and did not accept her responsibility to follow. The result: a fallen world. Talk about repercussions!

God gave man a will greater than our own to obey. God gave man work to do. God gave man a woman to love.

> 1 Corinthians 7:24: "Brothers, each man, as responsible to God, should remain in the situation God called him to."

In other words, get off the couch, people! Stop making excuses. Stop playing video games, feeling sorry for yourself, or drifting in pain. You were put here for a reason. Now do something! There is a time for rest. Biblically, even God rested on the Sabbath. But that is one day out of the week folks, not four, five, six, or even seven.

Men and women alike have a unique combination of talents/gifts and personality that give us all something to contribute while we are here on earth. This can be formal work, schooling to enhance various talents/gifts, volunteering, or anything other than doing nothing.

Each man and woman has a calling based on his or her talents/gifts and personality traits that we discussed in the previous chapter. Find your purpose-driven life at Dr. Rick Warren's website (http://www.purposedrivenlife.com/). No excuses, no regrets, men. Take responsibility for yourself, your wife, and your family. Yes, you will mess up from time to time. Simply admit it, state what you learned from it, and state what you will do differently next time. Then do it.

Being accountable is a related characteristic of accepting responsibility. We must admit when we are wrong, make amends as needed, and learn from the experience changing our future behavior for a better outcome. Making excuses and shifting responsibility by justifying our behavior by saying, "Well, at least I don't _____ (fill in the blank)" is part of what keeps us from receiving the inheritance of blessings, even if Christ is accepted.

Matthew 5:37: "Simply let your 'Yes' be 'Yes', and your 'No', 'No'; anything beyond this comes from the evil one."

Rejecting passivity and accepting responsibility also includes expressing four different emotions when appropriate to the situation.

1. King/queen – righteous (right thinking) energy, integrity.

2. Warrior – courageous (not afraid) energy, constructive purpose for fighting.

3. Lover – relational (faithful, loyal, and tender) energy, willing to be emotionally vulnerable.

4. Friend – relational (connecting/strengthening) energy, willing to encourage, challenge, and be accountable.

It is common to ask people what animal or characteristic they most identify with to better understand their personality. However, God calls us to be more than one dimensional. In fact, the four dimensions and examples of emotion are found everywhere in the Bible, and Christ exemplified them best! There is a situation in all of our lives where each one of these emotions is applied best too. So think about it the next time you reject passivity and accept responsibility.

INVEST ETERNALLY.

Malachi 3:10–12

Bring the whole tithe (10%) into the storehouse, that there may be food in my house. Test me in this, says the Lord Almighty, and see if I will not throw open the floodgates of heaven and pour out so much blessing that you will not have room enough for it. I will prevent pests from devouring your crops, and the vines in your fields will not cast their fruit says the Lord Almighty. Then all the nations will call you blessed, for yours will be a delightful land.

Tithing opens the windows to, and blessings from, heaven. It is the only place in the Bible that God invites testing Him. Keep in mind that tithing is only one component of investing eternally. Going to church, volunteering, teaching, mentoring, counseling, and conjoint couples therapy all count among others. Using any of the time, talents, and gifts God has bestowed on us is investing eternally.

Men and women who *cannot* tithe cannot afford not to. Tithing is simply an opportunity to obey God's blessing of paying us 10 percent too much. And even if we have accepted Christ, continue to work according to our talents and personality, but fail to invest eternally, we will not experience the full abundance of our inheritance.

Men and women, whether single, dating, married, divorced, father, stepfather/mother, grandfather/mother, great grandfather/mother: if you are unable or unwilling to accept Christ; reject passivity; accept responsibility to express king/queen, warrior, lover, and friend emotions and actions; and invest eternally; your abundant life table is unstable. And those trouble rocks will tip your abundant life table over! Chaos will characterize your life. Joy and the other fruits of the Spirit will not be experienced. Your blessings of abundance will be severely limited.

Think about It! Have you been able to identify authentic man and authentic woman from these four tenets? Are you applying/living all four tenets? What areas are opportunities for growth and improvement?

AUTHENTIC MARRIEDS

When the authentic man and authentic woman come together in marriage (or become authentic if already married), there is one more tenet of authenticity based on *leadership*. God's model for leadership is based on two specific actions found in Genesis 1:28

1. Create (Be fruitful and multiply and fill the earth …)

2. Cultivate (… and subdue it and have dominion over it.)

Creating incorporates the previous tenets of authentic manhood and womanhood ... rejecting passivity and accepting responsibility ... to create something meaningful and important. Cultivating is based on taking care of those creations and helping them to grow, thrive, and be sustained. Men are to lead courageously, and women are to *help* men lead courageously.

MEN ARE TO LEAD COURAGEOUSLY

In general, men are good at creating life, projects, and situations but fall short cultivating those lives, relationships, projects, and seeing them through. If men fail to be courageous leaders, chaos and pain will result. Adam failed to lead (In Genesis 1:16–17, God commanded Adam not to eat of only one tree; Eve was not made yet) and his wife Eve (created in Genesis 1:22) tempted him into sin probably because Adam was a poor communicator. But more importantly, he was not leading courageously.

The following leadership *to be's* and *not to be's* by Dale Carnegie help reinforce these courageous leadership tenets for men.[4]

Leadership To Be's (creators and cultivators)

1. Good leaders are to be sensitive to others needs.

2. Good leaders are to be affectionate toward people.

3. Good leaders are to be authentic.

4. Good leaders are to enthusiastically affirm other people.

Leadership Not To Be's (destroyers and neglectors)

1. Good leaders are *not* to be deceptive.

2. Good leaders are *not* to be people pleasers.

3. Good leaders are *not* to be greedy.

4. Good leaders are *not* to be self-serving.

Proverbs 18:22: "Whoever finds a wife finds something good and has obtained favor from the Lord."

WOMEN HELP MEN LEAD COURAGEOUSLY

The woman was taken from the side of man (from a rib) and designated the *helper* in the relationship. (See Genesis 1:21–22.) Now before everyone throws up the wall of resistance, *helper* does *not* mean less than, inferior, or any other derogatory inference. The colloquial saying, *Behind every great man stands an even greater woman,* certainly applies here. Follow along.

First, let us put the role of leadership (men) and support leadership (women) in context. If the man is the CEO (chief executive officer/ president) of the company, he cannot lead it alone (i.e., create and cultivate). He needs a vice president, treasurer, secretary, etc. That is why God said, "It is not good for man to be alone."

Since women are by nature better able to multitask, women who agree to assume these multiple roles are fully devoted to their role in helping their husbands lead. Both roles are necessary to succeed, to prosper in abundance!

Question: which role is most important in achieving the mission of the air force? The pilot? The ground crew? The flight control tower? The answer is obvious: none. They are all important, or the job cannot be completed.

The same principle applies to the marriage between husband and a wife. A husband who does not lead courageously and a wife who does not support his courageous leadership will simply result in chaos and problems.

Even Eve in the garden stepped outside her role as helping her husband lead and took it upon herself to lead them into sin. Again, the consequences were eternal.

If a man and a woman accept Christ, reject passivity, accept responsibility, and invest eternally, do the following Scripture words have less resistance or different meaning?

Ephesians 5:22–24: Wives, submit to your husbands as
to the Lord. For the husband is the head of the wife as
Christ is the head of the church, his body, of which he is
the Savior. Now as the church submits to their husbands
in everything.

Substitute the word *help* for *submit*. Does that make more sense?
Just because the husband is the head, it does not mean the wife is the
tail or feet to be trampled on. She is beside the husband, helping and
supporting courageous leadership. The husband is loving and protecting
the wife.

Ephesians 5:25–33: "Husbands, love your wives, just as
Christ loved the church and gave himself up for her."

Think about It! How is your marriage relationship with regard to
leadership? Are you leading courageously, men? Are you helping your
men lead courageously, women? What might happen if you do? What
might happen if you don't?

Answers to these "Think about It" questions can be characterized
in the following sections. Just remember that we must be an authentic
man and authentic woman first before we can be an authentic married
and experience *all* of the abundant blessings God has for us. This bears
repeating! If you are in a marriage and you (or your spouse) are *not*
authentic in one or more of the first four tenets (accept Christ, reject
passivity and accept responsibility, invest eternally) your life may look
like the following:

The Unauthentic Marrieds

First, we will likely see you in couples counseling, or you will
become another failed marriage statistic. We know this to be true as we
have been there ourselves. When one or both of the married couples are

subauthentic, the man will not lead courageously and the woman will not help the man lead courageously.

If you extrapolate the leadership tenet in a relationship where the man is authentic and the woman is not, the dynamics of the relationship changes, which increases stress and other problems. In essence, the man will have no leadership support and will be unable to do both jobs (president and vice president) effectively or efficiently. The same holds true if the woman is authentic and the man is not. She too cannot do both leadership jobs.

The characteristics of such relationships are grounded in chaos (disorder and confusion). Everyone is doing his or her own thing, including the children as applicable. There will be friction, fights, and a lot of unhappiness. They will live beyond your means and not tithe. They will not advance the kingdom by using their gifts and talents or investing eternally.

Men will be passive and have no internal drive/motivation, will not contribute to household chores, will not help with children, will not seek to improve themselves or their careers, will not ever want for more, and often will drink too much and play video games. There is financial stress, unhappiness, and general misery. These are the men who are miserable in their jobs and often blame their wives for not supporting them enough. They will make excuses for everything, and they do not feel their wives respect them.

Wives will want their husbands to step up and help more. Conversely, women who may become codependent for their men (i.e., make excuses for their lack of responsibility, poor work ethic, bad habits, etc.) are not actually supporting, or helping, their husbands. These women are often depressed, kid-centric, and stressed out. These wives are tired of excuses and do not feel loved, supported, or protected.

> Amos 3:3: "Do two people walk in the same direction (together) unless they have agreed to do so?"

The absence of one or more authentic manhood/womanhood tenet(s) results in each person walking in different directions and unable to resolve conflict. Divorce nearly always results over time. Abundant blessings are most certainly limited or absent entirely!

However, if you are in a marriage and you *are* authentic in all of the first four tenets (accept Christ, reject passivity and accept responsibility, invest eternally), your life may look like the following:

THE AUTHENTIC MARRIEDS

Authentic men and women experience a desire to invest eternally, tithe, and volunteer. They have purpose, responsibility, and a drive to always improve. They get stuff done and make good decisions. Men support their wives as their best friends, love them and their families and friends, and have peace. Women support their husbands in leadership and with encouragement and acceptance. They are both able to be king and queen, and they are warriors, lovers, and friends at the right times. They both know who they are supposed to be, and they are trying to be that person every day!

In order to stay on the same team and experience abundant blessings, the authentic marrieds are able to identify and overcome three problem areas proactively.

1. **Communication** problems start with an imbalance in biological wiring. Men do not talk nearly as much as women (fact). Neither listen as well as they should (95 percent of the time a person is thinking about himself or herself and not the other). We commonly misinterpret tone, nonverbal body language, and phrases that have context to us but not our partner since 90 percent is nonverbal in nature. Our needs, wants, and expectations are not delineated or expressed clearly. We do not follow up with the use of unconditional, positive, empathetic, clarifying remarks like "What I hear you saying is ..." We express emotion incorrectly, placing fault on the other as "You always make me feel ..." instead of saying, "I feel ABC when DEF happens."[38]

2. **Synergy** is the ideal goal for all conflict resolution. Saying, "Let's agree to disagree" to end an argument puts up a wall in the relationship, preventing oneness which leads to resentment and a hardening of the heart. Synergy is not compromise. *Compromise* sounds like the perfect solution but advocates two *half winners*. This method is far from ideal because it focuses on having both parties win a little so as to not lose a lot. This tends to reinforce agreement itself father than agreement on the best or most creative solution. Finally, in a compromise or accommodation solution, nobody comes out of the conflict feeling fully satisfied. *Synergy* is a win-win method based on identifying the personal interests or expectations behind each person's position. Synergy centers around good two-way communication getting both parties on the same page. The extra involvement by both parties will result in more effective or alternative solutions in which both parties feel like they have won without compromise.[39] In the end, both are able to say, "We agree this is best for both of us!"

3. **Common Goals** occur when communication is effective and synergy is the conflict resolution strategy. Every successful pro sports team, corporation, and couple has common goals they agree on and work toward. These goals revolve around a mission (what we are going to do) and vision (where we want to be) statement. The three biggest challenges (i.e., triad of uncommon goals) among couples revolve around sex, money, and family/kids:[40, 41, 42]

   a. **Sex.** Talk about it. We don't talk enough about sex with our partners for a variety of reasons (embarrassment, lack of experience/knowledge, cultural/religious stigmas, adolescent experiences, etc). We make a lot of assumptions about what our partner needs, wants, and expects, but we don't ask them. If your expectation of sex with your partner is framed by the what, when, where, how, and when criteria, make sure to delineate what is needed versus wanted. If your partner's primary love language is physical touch, they may actually need more than you if your primary love language is words of affirmation, for example. However, the blessing in love languages is that all five are grounded by sex as a physical touch, gift, act of service, affirmation, and quality time. Sex is a blessing (wedding gift) from God. It is not just of creating (making babies) but also for cultivating (healthy marital relationships). From four times a day to four times a month (i.e., normal healthy parameters), all things are permissible between a husband and wife as long as they agree and have a common goal communicated and agreed upon.

b. **Money.** Talk about it. Again, it becomes a problem because we don't talk about it enough with our partner for a variety of reasons (there isn't enough to go around, I am ashamed of my credit card debt, I like to spend money on frivolous things, etc.). Again, some of the differences about how money is spent, saved, and invested are grounded in our experience. If our parents had a budget and discussed it with us, we probably do as adults. If money was never talked about in our childhood homes or a source of constant argument, we will likely lean in those bents as well. A budget where both can find a set of common goals is invaluable. Set priorities. Hopefully tithing is one of them. Set bills (e.g., rent/house payment, insurance, and utilities) should also be at the top. Entertainment (movies, bowling, eating out, etc.) are not, however, essential and should be reserved for the lowest priority below savings and investments. Those who are not familiar with how to do this would almost certainly benefit from Dave Ramsey's "Financial Peace University" teachings and seminars on this topic (http://www.daveramsey.com/fpu/home/ictid/hp.newfpu.learnhow/).

    c. **Family/Kids.** Talk about it. Who is most important in the relationship? Parents, kids, cousins? Are you kid-centric? If you are or the spouse is not the most important (i.e., gets priority-needed attention over *all* others), there will be conflict. Note the emphasis on the word *needed.* A spouse who demands 100 percent of the spouse's attention at the expense of children or family needs for the sole purpose of self-gratification (i.e., narcissism) would be errant in this demand and expectation. However, for a husband and wife to become one, they must prioritize each other as most important second only to God—not soccer practice, Grandma's birthday party, etc. Therefore, if your spouse is not the most important person in the family/house, make a commitment to change. They need to be the most important or resentment again will creep in and harden even the most sensitive and beautiful heart.

Think about It! If you are not experiencing a joyful and abundant life as an authentic husband and wife, where might there be some imbalance? Communication; synergy; common goals for sex, money, family/kids?

BECOMING ONE FLESH

In order for husband and wife to become one flesh, men must be authentic and so must women. They must prioritize God first in their individual and married lives, followed by each other, and then lastly their children and extended family. If child/family wants and needs are more important than your spouses, there will be a problem. There is also a difference in the primary needs of men and women.[43]

1. **The #1 need of men is to feel respected.**

2. **The #1 need of women is to feel loved.**

If you do not know your love/respect language, and your spouse's (if applicable), please review the work by Gary Chapman:[44] There is a free online test you can also take (http://www.5lovelanguages.com/assessments/love/). The primary love/respect language communicates these needs more than any other (e.g., physical touch, acts of service, words of affirmation, receiving gifts, and quality time). Time must be committed to communicate and interact specific to the love/respect language.

Think about It! When did you last convey love/respect to another? How did you convey love/respect? Did the other person recognize the language you were using? What is your primary love language?

Part of feeling loved and respected also has to do with how we apologize to each other. Since we live in a fallen world and all sin, we have many opportunities in life to apologize to those we have wronged in order to reconcile the relationship. Be mindful that reconciliation is very different from forgiveness.

Forgiveness is to release ourselves from the prison of anger and resentment toward another who wronged us. Reconciliation is done for the benefit of both individuals involved in order to restore and redeem the relationship.

As with love languages, we also have preferred apology languages that we should all know. According to Gary Chapman,[45] the five language options are expressing regret, accepting responsibility, making restitution, genuinely repenting, and requesting forgiveness. The thirty-second quiz is free and worth taking at http://www.5lovelanguages.com/assessments/personal-profiles/apology/.

Think about It! When did you last apologize to a significant other? How did you convey the language of that apology? Did the other person recognize the language you were using? What is your primary apology language?

RECAP

Think about It! Do you know how to be an authentic man/woman? Do you know your love and apology language? Does your spouse? Are these things keeping you from experiencing the inheritance of joy and abundance in your life?

REMEMBER ...

Authentic Men and Women

1. **Accept Christ.**

2. **Reject passivity and accept responsibility.**

3. **Invest eternally.**

Authentic Marrieds:

4. **Men lead courageously and women help them lead!**

Remember marrieds that you are on the same team (one flesh)! Put your backs together and fight the Enemy together. So learn how, or be willing to learn! Find a mentor. Be mindful that we must be willing to learn and grow as much as we teach and foster growth. We cannot give others what we do not first possess ourselves. And we are all a process and so is everyone around us. So extend grace always!

CHAPTER 9

First the Natural

$\mathcal{I}$T IS NATURAL TO FOR us to place a lot of self-worth, value, and pride into the work we do. Most conversations start around what we do for a living or what we are going to school to be or do. It is something nearly everyone inherently understands is necessary to pay the bills. And yet job satisfaction is at the lowest point in the United States since the 1900s. Why?

The short answer is grounded in the fact that there is a very low reward (tangible and intangible alike) for the highest workload expectations ever! Add on the inability to change jobs or advance without advanced education and skill sets. Simply put, many feel trapped in their jobs and derive no satisfaction from their work whatsoever; even if they are doing a job using their talents and gifts. That is obviously the opposite of experiencing an abundant life.

What then?

KEEP SWIMMING

Two frogs fell into a deep cream bowl. One was an

optimist, but the other one took a gloomy view. "I shall drown and so will you," he cried. So with a last despairing cry, he closed his eyes and said good-bye. But the other frog, with a merry grin, said, "I cannot get out, but I won't give up. I will swim around till my strength is spent for having tried I will die content." Bravely he swam until it seemed his struggles churned the cream. On the top of newly formed butter, at last he stopped. And out of the bowl, he happily hopped.

What is the moral? It is easily found. If you can't get out, keep swimming around.

The popular kids story is the perfect one to exemplify (1 Corinthians 15:46: "The spiritual did not come first, but the natural, and after that the spiritual.")

One frog cried out but did nothing. The other frog did something. What was most natural to him was to swim. He swam and swam. Then the supernatural happened: cream formed to allow him the escape!

Hopefully by now you have realized some of your talents/gifts and your role as a man, woman, one-flesh couple. When lived out in the natural, supernatural abundance of God's blessing happens.

Genesis 26:12: "Isaac planted crops in that land and the same year reaped a hundredfold, because the LORD blessed him."

What was Isaac good at? Farming. He farmed; he prayed. He was blessed one hundred times as much as he invested! When? Within a year. That sounds pretty supernatural to me. That is the inheritance of abundance!

WORK FOR GOD, NOT MAN

The carpenter's story is a good illustration of why we should always think about our boss as God, not man. Hence, we should never cut corners.

Joe Smith was a loyal carpenter who worked nearly two decades for a successful contractor. One day, the contractor called him into his office and said, "Joe, I'm putting you in charge of the next house we build. I want you to order all the materials and oversee the job from the ground up." Joe accepted the assignment with great enthusiasm. He studied the blueprints and checked every measurement and specification. Suddenly, he had a thought. *If I am really in charge, why can't I cut a few corners, use less expensive materials, and put the extra money in my pocket? Who will know? Once the house is painted, it will look great.* So Joe went about his scheme. He ordered second-grade lumber and inexpensive concrete, put in cheap wiring, and cut every corner he could. When the home was finished, the contractor came to see it.

"What a fine job you have done" he said. "You have been such a faithful carpenter to me all these years that I have decided to show you my gratitude by giving to you this very house which you have built."

The moral of the story? Build well today. You may have to live with the results.

Dr. Jo and I are blessed with the gift of teaching. It comes natural to us and we truly love the teaching-learning process. We have done it all our adult lives in one form or fashion—currently as university professors. However, we have recently experienced a phenomenon associated with a generational and cultural shift that is well documented in the research literature. It is referred to generically as *customer entitlement*.[46] Simply put, many students (not all) no longer answer the question, "What do you want to get out of this class?" with verbiage about "Learning as much as I can so I can use it in the workplace or advance my career." Rather, they say, "To get an A." "Get or earn?" we ask? They reply, "Get!"

"The customer is always right" focus has replaced the traditional

DRS. ERIC & JOANNA OESTMANN

goal of academic quality and rigor in large part. This focus of customer entitlement also extends to a variety of other businesses in the twenty-first century.

"Give us your poor, your tired, your huddled masses yearning to breathe free." Sound like a job advertisement you recently responded to? Actually, this statement is engraved on the Statue of Liberty and yet it really describes many twenty-first century workers very well (i.e., poor, tired, and yearning).

This is partly why we are lobbying for a new DSM-V-TR (diagnostic and statistical manual of mental disorders) diagnosis "Worker Abuse Syndrome" to be recognized, and it may apply to many of you.[47]

Worker Abuse Syndrome (WAS) results from chronic exposure to being in a no-win position, being in a constant double bind, being told to do one thing over and over, and being held to one set of rules and then being asked to break all of them for the customer. It occurs when you are held accountable for things beyond your direct control. It occurs when organizational leaders do not actually lead but react to each customer irrationally and illogically. It occurs when leaders view subordinates as a "dime a dozen" (i.e., no real value to the organization, but rather a necessary evil). The message is clear: "If you don't _____, there are plenty more like you that will take your place."

These experiences result in constant fear. The individual startles easily, tensing up when they open e-mail, listen to phone messages, or interact with customers and colleagues alike. The results of chronic exposure to this environment cause the employee to become emotionally numb. A lack of caring creeps in. Employees become irritable, more aggressive, or complacent. Ultimately, "learned helplessness" occurs.

Learned helplessness is a motivational problem where the employee begins to believe they are incapable to do anything in order to improve their performance or meet employer and customer expectations. Dr. Lenore Walker characterized learned helplessness as a series of events that result in employees no longer wanting to try to improve but just marking time.[48]

Anxiety and depression often co-occur. See if you recognize any of the following symptoms.

WORKER ABUSE SYNDROME

A. The person has been exposed to a traumatic work event in which both of the following were present:

1. The person experienced, witnessed, or was confronted with a work event or events that involved actual or threatened unemployment, retaliation, or a threat to the personal integrity of self or others.

2. The person's response involved intense hopelessness, helplessness, or horror.

B. The traumatic work event is persistently re-experienced in one (or more) of the following ways:

1. Recurrent and intrusive distressing recollections of the work event, including images, thoughts, or perceptions.

2. Recurrent distressing work-related dreams of the event.

3. Acting or feeling as if the traumatic work event were recurring.

4. Intense psychological distress at exposure to internal or external cues that symbolize or resemble an aspect of the traumatic work event.

5. Physiological reactivity on exposure to internal or external work cues that symbolize or resemble an aspect of the traumatic event.

C. Persistent avoidance of work stimuli associated with the trauma and numbing of general responsiveness (not present before the trauma), as indicated by three (or more) of the following:

1. Efforts to avoid thoughts, feelings, or conversations associated with the work trauma.

2. Efforts to avoid work activities, places, or students that arouse recollections of the trauma.

3. Inability to recall an important aspect of the work trauma.

4. Markedly diminished interest or participation in significant work activities and lack of passion in work and teaching.

5. Feeling of detachment or estrangement from customers, colleagues, and supervisors.

6. Restricted range of affect (e.g., unable to have kind, loving feelings).

7. Sense of a foreshortened future (e.g., does not expect to have a job, contract, or career).

D. Persistent symptoms of increased work arousal (not present before the work trauma), as indicated by two (or more) of the following:

1. Difficulty falling or staying asleep.

2. Irritability or outbursts of anger.

3. Difficulty concentrating.

4. Hypervigilance on and off line.

5. Exaggerated startle response.

E. Duration of the disturbance (symptoms in criteria B, C, and D) is more than one month.

F. The disturbance causes clinically significant distress or impairment in social, occupational, or other important areas of functioning.

Think about It! As an employee, have you ever felt like you were caught between a rock and a hard place? Can't make anyone happy? No matter what you do, how hard you work, or how great the activities you choose to do in your class, someone inevitably complains and hates what you do? Have you ever felt like it just does not matter what you do, because it will result in someone complaining? Do you have WAS? What are you going to do to not let the Enemy win?

Closely related to burnout, WAS is becoming increasingly common and perhaps you can identify with it. However, it can be overcome! Parker Palmer's book *The Courage to Teach* provides a practical *what to do* list to overcome.[49]

1. Recognize it when you start to experience it.

2. Understand it is part of the Enemy's plan to steal your joy, kill your career, and destroy your passion.

3. Make a conscious decision to shift your focus to working for God, not man.

4. Keep using your natural gifts/talents until God does the supernatural.

5. Understand that we are salt and light to the fallen world and there is a purpose for earnest toil.

6. Recognize that if we shortchange our boss in the natural, we shortchange God's blessings in the supernatural.

7. Know that we may have to live with the results of our natural actions.

For us, #7 is particularly meaningful. Simply put, if we were to stay in WAS mode, our students would not have the opportunity to learn, critically think, and ultimately contribute to society. If we look forward in time, students who do not advance the knowledge necessary in higher education will only detract from their needed competence in the natural, thereby supporting the Enemy's goals. For example, we don't want counseling psychology students to graduate without the knowledge they need to provide competent care to others who may be our loved ones, friends, or ourselves. Therefore, we make a conscious choice every day to work for God, not man, and use the talents/gifts to their fullest. Of course, some days it is easier to apply this than others!

Also, remember, that the hundredfold supernatural blessing is a real possibility when we keep doing the natural first. Again, that is part of our inheritance promise of joyful abundance! So keep dreaming big while you work in the natural.

RECAP

Think about It! Are you going to let the symptoms of WAS dictate your natural (gift/talent) contributions and shortchange the supernatural blessings? Are you able to see the value in working for God, not man, no matter what the situation?

REMEMBER ...

First the natural (believing and confessing Christ is Lord) and then the supernatural (eternal life in heaven with Him, and abundant blessings until that day). Remember if you have never felt like quitting, you were probably never running the race in the first place. Just keep swimming and remember you work for God, not man, so expect great rewards!

PART 4

For the Glory of Him!

If you remain in me and my words remain in you, ask whatever you wish, and it will be done for you. This is to my Father's glory, that you bear much fruit, showing yourselves to be my disciples.

John 15:7–8

CHAPTER 10

What Makes God Look Good?

N o, GOD DOES NOT HAVE a self-image problem. What better way to introduce salvation opportunities to an unsaved world than to have your children share the fruit of the Spirit?

> Galatians 5:22–23: "But the fruit of the Spirit is love, joy, peace, forbearance, kindness, goodness, faithfulness, gentleness and self-control. Against such things there is no law."

If you think about the people in your life that you most enjoy spending time with, I think you will recognize the fruit. They love and are happy, peaceful, patient, kind, good, faithful, gentle, and in control. This is by definition the *salt and light* the world so desperately needs. In the natural, we are drawn to food that has taste and is colorful. The more colorful the food, the healthier it typically is. The same analogy extends to God's children.

Think about it in earthly terms. Whether you have children or not, it is natural to be proudest of our children's accomplishments of success, not mediocrity. For example, most parents were very proud of their child's graduation day, compared with the day-in-and-day-out going-to-school days. The diploma was the reward for all of the day-to-day hard work. The diploma also signifies an opportunity to apply that knowledge for the benefit of others.

Extending the analogy, if we were awarded a diploma every day (fruit) and used it to benefit others, isn't that the pinnacle of making our heavenly Father look good? Yes!

The abundant life makes God look good. The abundant life is characterized by success, not failure. The abundant life is full of fruit! How much fruit?

....

John 15:8: "This is to my Father's glory, that you bear much fruit."

....

Much fruit! Not a little fruit or some fruit but much fruit! The fruit of the Spirit overflowing in our lives makes God look good. In *The Purpose Driven Life* by Rick Warren, the ultimate answer to "Why are we here?" is found by understanding that our overall purpose is to "make God look good." In other words, "to glorify Him"!

God doesn't want his kids running around looking like ragamuffins. He doesn't look good when His kids blow their inheritance on booze, gambling, and other meaningless stuff. He wants us to obey His word, be patient (there is an appointed time and place), and use our gifts/talents (in the natural) to glorify Him!

One of the first references to what Glorifies Him is found in Luke 2 when the shepherds were visited by an angel of the Lord and told the Christ child was born. After the shepherds visit, they left to spread the word about this child, "glorifying and praising God for all the things they had heard and seen" (v. 20). The shepherds told others. Therefore, telling others about Christ (also known as the Great Commission), either by our words or actions, glorifies God and produces fruit.

As succinctly as possible, to glorify God, all we really need to ask is, "What would Jesus do?" Yes, WWJD? He would probably say please and thank-you, smile and laugh, sing and praise, be nice and not mean, be selfless and not selfish. The list goes on, of course.

Think about It! What fruit are you producing?

PRODUCE MORE FRUIT!

John Wooden was the UCLA basketball coach from 1963 to 1975. He won ten out of twelve NCAA championships and coached the likes of Kareem Abdul Jabar and Bill Walton, among others, and is a long-time success guru. According to him, successful leaders must learn to be far more concerned with empowerment than with power. One way to live empowered is to embrace and expect change with an attitude of learning something new every day.

1. Define the vision of who you want to be.

2. Determine how you will best achieve that vision.

3. Live out the vision every day as you transform vision into reality.

Dr. Phil McGraw[15, 16] encourages individuals who want a real commitment to self-improvement to adopt life laws-life decisions. Several of the ones directly related to making God look good through acts of obedience, patience, and gift/talent utilization include the following:

» I will live my life with integrity.

» I will not resort to physical or verbal violence.

» I will be less selfish and think of others first.

» I will not complain or condemn.

» I will take care of myself so that I can take care of my family.

» I will not feel empty or alone; God is my one essential friend.

» I will spend quality time with my family, because time cannot be regenerated.

» I will not program myself for failure.

» I will do what it takes and be committed in order to have what I want.

» I will not be frustrated by life.

» I will enjoy the good and tolerate the bad, and move forward.

» I will not insist on always being right.

» I will take action to make my family's life better.

» I will not take my family for granted, because they are a priceless gift.

» I will expect change and not be paralyzed by fear.

» I will not be bound by the chains of hatred, anger, and resentment.

» I will forgive in order to have my freedom.

» I will not make excuses but accept accountability for my actions.

» I will evaluate my life often and take action to avoid a rut.

» I will not avoid risk or fear rejection.

» I will give myself a chance and insist on results.

» I will not settle or rationalize why I do not want or deserve more.

» I will work smart and play more.

» I will not waste my God-given talents and gifts.

» I will set personal, relational, professional, and spiritual goals.

» I will not let past events control my future.

» I will live with God in my family and thank Him for our blessings.

» I will not expect that the world owes me anything.

» I will work on obtaining our desires by actively living and pursuing the abundant life.

Think about It! Do any of the above life laws-life decisions sound like something that would produce more fruit in your life?

RECAP

Think about It! What areas of obedience, patience, and gift/talent utilization might we want to improve in order to make God look good?

REMEMBER ...

The more fruit you produce, the better God looks! It is a win-win synergy scenario of abundant blessings.

CHAPTER 11

Reconciliation and Redemption

THERE IS A FUNDAMENTAL DIFFERENCE between forgiveness and reconciliation. Forgiveness frees us from the bondage of anger toward another. (In other words, it is for our benefit primarily.) Reconciliation, on the other hand, is reserved for those who are truly worth the time and energy to heal a wound that has prevented a joyful and abundant relationship between the two individuals. (In other words, it is for the benefit of both parties.) Therefore, reconciliation only occurs when both parties who are hurt are willing to work toward a common goal of more than just forgiveness. Sometimes, reconciliation needs a miracle to occur. Other times, the miracle is reconciliation. Similarly, redemption is always a miracle that glorifies God. And this chapter will share with you two very heartfelt miracles. One of reconciliation. One of redemption.

Think about It! When was the last time you forgave someone? How did that make you feel? When was the last time you reconciled with someone? How did that make both of you feel? Is reconciliation always possible, or are there some you simply need to love from a distance?

MIRACLE OF RECONCILIATION

Proverbs 22:6: "Start children off on the way they should go, and even when they are old they will not turn from it."

If you have strong-willed children, you will know this Scripture in Proverbs by heart. The highlighted word to focus on here is *should*. That obviously does not mean they will go in the way we parents want them to. Case in point, when you blend a family after divorce and remarriage, one of the most painful experiences involves one of the worst forms of child abuse: parental alienation syndrome (PAS). And we have experienced it firsthand.

> For, in the final analysis, our most basic common link is that we all inhabit this small planet. We all breathe the same air. We all cherish our children's future. And we all are mortal.
>
> John F. Kennedy, Commencement Address, American University, June 11, 1963

We (parents) *all* "cherish our children's future." In short, we want our children's lives to be better than our own. We want to impart knowledge, wisdom, and love based on our own learning experiences so our children will have a better, more fulfilling life. We begin the parental journey with an idealistic vision in our heads.

Most parents remember the exact day our children said, "Mommy" or "Dadda." It was at that moment we were somehow recognized as parents by our infant children. The joy of first words, first steps, first everything.

Divorce is not something we believe any parent is thinking when they choose to have children. And yet divorce is a reality in 50–60 percent of all marriages. Yes, the children suffer the pangs of divorce that they did not cause. Children do not need to suffer the abuse of a parent driven to alienate him or her from the other parent, and yet some do suffer that pain.

We learn early that life on this planet was never meant to be easy by the Divine Creator. We are told things like, "What doesn't kill you makes you stronger" and "God never gives you more than you can handle." There are bumps in the road, pain and suffering, and difficult situations that each person experiences on the journey of life. Some occur as the result of our own doing, while others have no logical reason or rationale.

We know that people experience pain related to physical ailments/ diseases, financial loss/challenges, legal issues, career-related trauma, relationship distress, and a variety of other sources. However, there is one painful experience that we would not wish on our worst enemy and certainly not ourselves. There is one painful experience that tests eternal truths and breaks even the strongest of hearts into a million pieces ...

The death of a child who appears alive, but is truly unrecognizable to the parent, is the result of parental alienation syndrome. Dr. Richard A. Gardner, MD, clinical professor of child psychiatry, is the foremost expert on PAS. According to Gardner, the parent alienator (inflicting alienation on the other parent) is often characterized as a narcissist, psychopath, and emotional blackmailer who has low self-esteem, depressive symptoms, and substance-abuse issues. However, there are eight primary characteristics of PAS according to Gardner.[50]

1. A campaign of denigration of one parent by the other parent.

2. Weak, absurd, or frivolous rationalizations for the deprecation of one parent by the other parent.

3. Lack of ambivalence.

4. The *independent-thinker* phenomenon.

5. Reflexive support of the alienating parent in the parental conflict.

6. Absence of guilt over cruelty to and/or exploitation of the alienated parent.

7. The presence of borrowed scenarios.

8. Spread of animosity to the friends and/or extended family of the alienated parent.

PAS exists on a spectrum from mild to severe types based on the degree to which the above eight characteristics are manifest. Brainwashing occurs in which the target parent is systematically and consciously programmed by the other parent to denigrate them. The target parent is vilified in every way possible. In short, children are programmed to hate the targeted parent and speak to the alienated parent with every vilification and profanity in their vocabulary, without embarrassment or guilt. In Pamela Richardson's book *A Kidnapped Mind*, her child Dash frequently, almost automatically, responded to his mother with vulgar and inappropriate statements that were completely untrue.[51]

The process of PAS occurs over time. Like the frog that is placed in a pan of water with the heat slowly being turned up, there comes a point when the frog is dead because of the water's heat. Children exposed to PAS eventually die. They become a shell of a human being. They are zombies, dead but alive at the same time. They are programmed, brainwashed, and completely different from the child you raised. They are abused emotionally, psychologically, and physically beyond what most humans could conjure up in their worst nightmare. While with PAS it is more common for mothers alienating their children from their fathers, it is also experienced by fathers alienating their children from their mothers, according to Gardner.

We have experienced PAS in both capacities and will share with you the telltale signs and situations to be ever vigilant of. While we wish we could say that seeing these signs will allow you to intervene successfully and prevent PAS, it is certainly not a guarantee. Rather, identifying any of the signs of PAS will more likely provide you an opportunity to see what is coming. Perhaps you can successfully stave off the results of

PAS. If so, it should be considered the greatest gift a parent can receive and give to their children in that situation.

While it sounds hopeless, there is some comfort knowing you are not alone in this experience. It is our sincerest hope that by sharing our story of PAS, that you will find something that helps. Whether you are the dad or mom, stepdad or stepmom, or family member who experiences PAS, we have been there! We are still there to some degree, but reconciliation is emerging.

Our story of PAS began several years after becoming a blended family. It took that long to fully recognize PAS, although the abuse and precursors to abuse had begun long before. One day our children, teenagers, were no longer recognizable as human beings who are able to experience empathy, sympathy, or any other real emotion toward the parents who raised them. Parents who are made to feel crazy and at fault, but who are clearly not.

It is important to recognize the fact that the alienated parent did not do anything to deserve it! Let me repeat: you did *not* do anything to deserve this abuse. It was *not* because you chose divorce or divorce was chosen for you. However, according to Gardner, the adversarial system of the courts related to divorce and custody arrangements often precipitates PAS.

Anyone who has experienced divorce knows firsthand the adversarial system of law in this country. Despite the most common reason given for divorce being *irreconcilable differences*, the term implies two people simply going on with life in separate ways. The reality when children are involved is something else entirely. It is battle after battle over everything and nothing. It is a war that is only won by the attorneys getting paid for their time.

What is in the child's best interest becomes the battle cry of both parents and their lawyers. The more adversarial the divorce, the more likely PAS will occur.

In its broadest sense, shape-shifting occurs when a being (usually human) either has the ability to change its shape into that of another person, creature, or other entity or when a being finds its shape involuntarily changed by someone else. If the shape change is voluntary, its cause may be an act of will, a magic word or magic words, a potion, or a magic object. If the change is involuntary, its cause may be a curse or spell; a wizard's, magician's or fairy's help; a deity's will; a temporal change, such as a full moon or nightfall; love; or death. The transformation may or may not be purposeful.

PAS causes your children to shape-shift. They become unrecognizable to the parent being alienated. The child sees anything other than meanness as a betrayal to the alienating parent.

It is important to remember that while we feel hurt, and we are the victim of PAS, the children are too. Amy Baker compiled a book entitled *Adult Children of Parental Alienation Syndrome* from interviews conducted with forty adult children who were part of the PAS process ranging in age from nineteen to sixty-seven years of age (fifteen were male and twenty-five were female).[52,53] This is a unique viewpoint from the children who are now adults. Baker's conclusions revealed the following:

1. The child did not realize he or she was being brainwashed by the other parent.

2. The child still feels like the alienated parent should have done more for him or her.

3. The child still feels like he or she is betraying the alienating parent when he or she spends time with the alienated parent.

Together, we are committed to find a way to better understand, prevent, and minimize the damage caused by PAS.

WHAT TO DO IN THE NATURAL?

One of the challenges here is to understand the application of forgiveness versus reconciliation when it comes to Jesus' command to *love God and love people*. Sometimes, you have to love people from a distance. Reconciliation certainly glorifies God, and love is the main ingredient.

Simply love your children through the alienation process; oftentimes at a distance. Pray for them. Pray for yourself. Praise Him in this storm! Always keep God first. Remember your children are God's too. Believe there is an appointed time and place where reconciliation will occur. Remember you, the alienated parent, did nothing to deserve it! Support the alienated current spouse and extend as much grace and patience as possible. Find a great licensed therapist to talk with. They can help keep you grounded in reality when the surreal experience of PAS occurs. Then grieve.[53]

The grief process is well documented and supported with the literature. Kubler-Ross's five stages of grief model (denial, anger, bargaining, negotiation, and acceptance) were developed initially as a model for helping dying patients to cope with death and bereavement of loved ones and even pets. However, the concept also provides insight and guidance for coming to terms with personal trauma and change, and for helping others with emotional adjustment and coping, even PAS. Recognize first that grief is an individual process. The five stages were note meant to be a rigid series of sequential or uniformly timed steps.

By way of example, people do not always experience all of the five grief-cycle stages. Some stages might be revisited. Some stages might not be experienced at all. Transition between stages can be more of an ebb and flow rather than a progression. The five stages are not linear; nor are they equal in their experience. People's grief reactions to emotional trauma are as individual as their fingerprints.

In this sense, you might wonder what the purpose of the model is if it can vary so much from person to person. An answer is that the model acknowledges there to be an individual pattern of reactive emotional responses, which people feel when coming to terms with death, bereavement, and great loss or trauma, etc. The model recognizes that people have to pass through their own individual journey of coming to terms with the loss, after which there is generally an acceptance of reality, which then enables the person to cope.

Identifying the new reality of our lives and relationships is the miracle of reconciliation from PAS. It is living in every moment, no matter how small or how brief. It is watching your children become adults often from the sideline, but still being able to watch every now and again. It is being able to move on with your own hopes and dreams.

Reconciliation is being able to help others who have experienced and are currently experiencing PAS. Reconciliation is peace knowing that you did everything in your power you could and that you are never giving up on them and their success.

Was it our plan? Obviously not. Was it what we thought was best? Obviously not. However, we trust God has a plan for our best and our adult children's best. But also remember back to our earlier discussion on logotherapy and not trying to answer *why*, but rather to try to see *to what ends*.

There were some identifiable *to what ends* positives in this pain. First, we were truly able to put God first and each other second in our lives. Children were finally put in the order to which God designed them to be in importance. We were able to focus on each other, advance our careers through a more flexible travel schedule, and attend a plethora of continuing education seminars to not only help us work through it but to help others as well. We are confident that there will be many more "to what ends" positives in our lifetime as well.

MIRACLE OF REDEMPTION

1 Peter 5:10: "And the God of all grace, who called you to his eternal glory in Christ, after you have suffered a little while, will himself restore you and make you strong, firm and steadfast."

In 2012, Dr. Eric wrote a screenplay entitled *Redemption*. It is based on a true story that exemplifies the miracle of redemption only possible by the supernatural grace of God. In order to protect the individuals' private lives, we are purposefully changing their names to fictitious ones.

The story begins with a husband and wife who are characterized as successful and prosperous. They both have professional careers, multiple properties, multiple vehicles, high social status in the community, and love each other. They look like they have it all, but Jesus is not a priority. Remember that God loves us too much to leave us alone and sometimes He gets our attention in extreme ways.

In the middle of the day, the phone rings. It is Mark's business partner calling his wife Jennifer. "Mark was arrested this morning. The FBI says he is a fugitive and kept calling him a different name."

Of course, Jennifer has no idea what is going on until FBI agents knock on her door and explain. Mark was wanted in connection with the most notorious and successful bank robbery gang in North America in the twentieth century, The Stopwatch Gang. A man on the run from the Canadian authorities for nearly forty years was finally caught by the FBI in Fort Lauderdale, Florida. A man that never told his wife what his real name was. As you can imagine, Jennifer's life crumbled all around her.

Betrayal, anger, denial, and more anger consumed her. Lawyers were hired and assets were frozen and then confiscated by the feds. Questions had no answers as Mark was kept in Miami-Dade jail for more than two years without the ability to explain the truth to his wife. For two long years, Jan lived with the pain and humiliation plastered on TV, newspapers, and other media outlets.

Jennifer's search to find out who she married took her to Canada, South America, San Diego, Sedona, and back to Florida. The journey was physically dangerous, emotionally exhausting, and financially draining. In the end, Jennifer was left with nothing but partial answers and a lot more pain.

Her professional reputation was tarnished. Her finances were depleted. Her car was seized by the government. Her house had been confiscated by the government. Her husband remained silent awaiting trial and extradition to Canada. Divorce papers were finally signed, and then she hit rock bottom. No hope for reconciliation or redemption, just dark shadows and mere existence.

But a shadow does not exist without some light. Even in the deepest valleys. Again, there are ultimately two choices: give up or press on. Jennifer's resilience allowed her to search for meaning. To what end can we make sense of this? The answer can come only from the perspective that *all things work together for our good.* And first things first, that requires us to resolve the quintessential crisis of faith where our belief in Jesus must also include action confessing our acceptance of Jesus. Pillar #1 of authentic womanhood complete.

Fortunately, the redemption blessing is possible with Christ in our corner advocating for us. The redemption blessing melted away the pain and distrust over time as the additional pillars of authentic womanhood are being put into place. Rejecting passivity, accepting responsibility, and investing eternally become daily intentional practices. Little did Jennifer know, but Mark was becoming an authentic man at the same time some three thousand miles away in Ottawa, Canada.

Then, a leap of faith: a move to Canada, a love restored, and a marriage remade in God's time and place were just a tip of the iceberg of blessings. New careers were immediately successful and prosperous. More importantly, love really did conquer all! The words of the Kerrie Roberts song ring true.

> No matter what, I'm gonna love You. No matter what,
> I'm gonna need You. I know that You can find a way to
> keep me from the pain, but if not, if not, I'll trust you,
> no matter what, no matter what.

When a couple can experience the ultimate betrayal and loss but accept Christ in the process, find the assuredness of eternal life, become authentic man and woman, and then authentic marrieds, they go from a 0 to a 100 on the Marital Happiness Scale. That is a redemption blessing indeed!

MARITAL HAPPINESS SCALE

(Adapted from Azrin, N.; Naster, B.; and Jones, R. (1973).
"Reciprocity Counseling: A Rapid Learning-Based Procedure for
Marital Counseling." *Behaviour Research and Therapy*, 11.)

This scale is intended to estimate your current happiness with your marriage on each of the ten dimensions listed. You are to circle one of the numbers (1–10) beside each marriage area.

Ask yourself this question as you rate each marriage area: "If my partner continues to act in the future as he /she is acting today with respect to this marriage area, how happy will I be I be with this area of our marriage?" In other words, state according to the numerical scale (1–10) exactly how you feel today. Try to exclude all feelings of yesterday and concentrate only on the feelings of today in each of the marital areas. Also, try not to allow one category to influence the results of the other categories.

Total your points out of 100 possible. If you are less than 70 total (or 7/10 in any one area) a tune up is likely needed. We strongly urge finding a Christian licensed counselor in your state to make an appointment with if that is the case.

Rate on a 10 point scale	1 = Completely Unhappy to 10 = Completely Happy
Household responsibilities	
Rearing of children	
Social activities	
Money	
Communication	
Sex	
Academic or Occupational progress	
Personal independence	
Spouse independence	
General happiness	
Total: X out of 100 possible	

Think about It! How would you react when faced with PAS? How about the worst kind of spousal betrayal? Would you be able to focus on the miracles of reconciliation and redemption that glorify Him?

REMEMBER ...

The greater the tragedy, the greater the triumph of reconciliation and redemption that glorifies Him!

CHAPTER 12

Transformation

*U*NSAVED TO SAVED. *POOR TO* rich. *Cursed to blessed. Sinner to saint. Stumbling blocks to stepping-stones. Test to testimony.* The dichotomies of transformation can all be summarized generically as going from unsuccessful to successful. And this transformation (no longer conforming to the pattern of this world: Romans 12:2) is made available to us through the inheritance of abundance for success and prosperity!

FOUR-DIMENSIONAL BEINGS

We exist in four dimensions: (biological, psychological, social, and spiritual). If one or more dimension is unhealthy, or lacking, transformation becomes impeded.

BIOLOGICAL

Your body is a temple and should be cared after.

1 Corinthians 6:19–20: Do you not know that your body is a temple of the Holy Spirit, who is in you, whom you have received from God? You are not your own; you were bought at a price. Therefore, honor God with your body.

Sometimes, we need help with our temple. Health-care professionals, medications, and technology are all gifts of God to help us optimize and heal our physical bodies.

PSYCHOLOGICAL

Take all thoughts captive.

2 Corinthians 10:4–5: The weapons we fight with are not the weapons of the world. On the contrary, they have divine power to demolish strongholds. We demolish arguments and every pretension that sets itself up against the knowledge of God, and we take captive every thought to make it obedient to Christ.

Sometimes, we need help with taking thoughts captive. We have a lot of help available through professional counselors, psychologists/psychiatrists, medications, and other medical professionals.

SOCIAL

God did not intend for us to be alone.

Proverbs 27:17: "As iron sharpens iron, so one person sharpens another."

Note the gender neutrality in this verse. Men need to be with other men. Women need to be with other women too. Find those who-saids!

SPIRITUAL

There are some obstacles to our spiritual health that are common and grounded in religion. Make sure to separate religion from Christianity here. An example in the Bible that is one of the few instances where Jesus actually got angry was not with the sinner but with the Levites/religious leaders of the day.

Matthew 21:12: Jesus entered the temple courts and drove out all who were buying and selling there. He overturned the tables of the money changers and the benches of those selling doves.

Jesus recognized the obstacles religion placed in the way of a relationship with Him! One obstacle many of us still have not resolved today is based on a *fear* of God.

Fear God has had a longstanding negative connotation that the church promoted in the past as a way to control people, influence politics, and gain power. It implies that if we are not *towing the line*, God will smite us with punishments. Fact: there is a long list of punishments spelled out in the Old Testament book of Leviticus. Good news, the New Testament (new promise) replaces the Old Testament, and those punishments have already paid through the blood of Jesus Christ.

If we use *Strong's Concordance* and search the root word meanings of *fear*, we will find that the term *know* is much more congruent with the intention of that phrase applicable in the twenty-first century we live in and in English language. If we replace the word *fear* with *know*, how does that change the more than three hundred verses (depending on your Bible version) that you have read over the years? Read them again replacing the word *fear* with *know* as applicable. How does that change your view of God?

How can we take delight in the Lord if we fear Him? Sounds like an abundance blocker to us.

Psalm 37:4: "Take delight in the Lord, and he will give you the desires of your heart."

Think about It! Are we still afraid of God? Is fear limiting the abundant life experiences?

A Servant's Prayer for Success

In the Bible, there is only *one* official prayer to God for *success*. A prayer made by a man with no name. A man who was a faithful servant to Abraham. A prayer impacting every generation since.

What is this prayer you may ask? It is found in the obscurity of Genesis 24:12-14:

> The he prayed, "O Lord, God of my master Abraham, give me success today, and show kindness to my master Abraham. See I am standing beside this spring, and the daughters of the townspeople are coming out to draw water. May it be that when I say to a girl, 'Please let down your jar that I may have a drink', and she says, "Drink, and I'll water your camels too'—let her be the one you have chosen for your servant Isaac. By this I will know that you have shown kindness to my master."

The purpose of the prayer is obvious: to give the servant success in finding a wife for his master's son, Isaac. This servant's task was assigned by Abraham, who wanted him to find his son a specific spouse. A spouse that was *not* from the daughters of the Canaanites.

Why did Abraham specify a wife not of Canaanite descent? Because Abraham knew he messed up when he jumped ahead of God's promise and conceived a child with his maidservant Hagar at the urging of his wife Sarah. Ishmael was the result of this sin and the fork in the road between Islam and Christianity. Only later did he and Sarah conceive a child, "Isaac," at the ripe old age of one hundred. Therefore, any wife from a sinful lineage would not be successful or honorable in God's sight.

The story is quite lengthy, but Abraham's servant had not even completed the prayer when Rebekah answered the prayer. Nobody can say God doesn't answer prayers quickly. Although this is not often the case, it is one example of transformative expediency by God.

Rebekah was the wife God chose for Isaac. The result of this marriage was two sons: Esau and Jacob. You know, Jacob the *father of Israel.* The father of the twelve tribes of Israel. The direct lineage of Jesus Christ through his earthly father Joseph, who was descended from Solomon, David, and Judah (one of the original twelve sons of Jacob).

Do you now see how important this prayer for success was? The result: salvation of the entire world!

The servant's prayer for success was ultimately God's success. Do you now see why God answered it so quickly?

Therefore, let us pray.

> Heavenly Father, please grant me success in this world, for it is ultimately Your success. By this I will know Your kindness to me and to the world. In Jesus' name, amen.

Think about It! Doesn't God want us to be successful, transformed?

A SERVANT'S PRAYER FOR PROTECTION

Get dressed every morning by putting on the full suit of holy armor. After all, life on earth is a battle every day.

> Ephesians 6:12: For our struggle is not against flesh and blood, but against the rulers, against the authorities, against the powers of this dark world and against the spiritual forces of evil in the heavenly realms.

The word *battle* appears in the Bible more than two hundred times. Another thing God thought we should know more about! We are battling principalities of darkness here on earth. An enemy described as a roaring lion seeking to devour. But there is good news.

Romans 8:31: "If God is for us, who can be against us?"

So we should put on the full armor of God so we can stand against the Devil's schemes.

Ephesians 6:14–18: Stand firm then, with the belt of truth buckled around your waist, with the breastplate of righteousness in place, and with your feet fitted with the readiness that comes from the gospel of peace. In addition to all this, take up the shield of faith, with which you can extinguish all the flaming arrows of the evil one. Take the helmet of salvation and the sword of the Spirit, which is the word of God. And pray in the Spirit on all occasions with all kinds of prayers and requests. With this in mind, be alert and always keep on praying for all the Lord's people.

This is something we do every day! You can too. Get dressed with the armor of God.

Therefore, let us pray.

Heavenly Father, get us dressed each day with the belt of truth (the grace and mercy of Jesus), the breastplate of righteousness (right thinking), the shield of faith (confident trust in You), the sword of the Spirit (Your word and guidance), the helmet of salvation (eternal life and health, wealth, and wisdom here on earth), and the shoes of peace (fruit of the Spirit and success in all we do). In Jesus' name, amen.

Think about It! Doesn't God want us to be protected from the Evil One?

A SERVANT'S PRAYER FOR TRANSFORMATION

In the Sermon on the Mount, when Jesus stated, "Blessed are the poor," many of us quit reading and concluded that poverty and poor people should be happy. After all, *blessed* means "happy."

The rest of Jesus' instruction was this: "Blessed are the poor in spirit." For some reason we forget about the *in spirit* part and simply assume that Jesus was himself a poor carpenter's son. But the question is, was he?

No, far from it. Jesus was, after all, the King of King's son. Wise men blessed him and his family with gifts estimated to be in excess of several million dollars in today's terms. Jesus' disciples were also quite wealthy. Consider Matthew, the tax collector, who was able to entertain three hundred guests in his house for a party. I know very few people who can accommodate three hundred guests for a party. It must have been quite a house! James and John were the sons of Zebedee, a very wealthy businessman. Simon, called Peter, was a wealthy and successful fisherman.

God wants us to be successful too. God left us His last will and testament. After all, we are God's children and have done nothing to deserve these gifts other than accept Jesus as our Lord and Savior. By grace, we are therefore entitled.

Prosperity is more than just financial wealth. However, financial wealth is an easy measure, objective, tangible, and often used to illustrate many success principles and stories.

Everyone would like to receive an inheritance, but only a select few actually get one from their earthly fathers. Few truly understand that we are *all* entitled to an inheritance of abundance from our heavenly Father. Another obstacle to overcome is learning that our inheritance of abundance (anointing of prosperity/success) has three conditions:

1. At an appointed time and place.

2. Using our talents and gifts.

3. For the glory of Him.

Perhaps the quote by Philip Yancey is true: "I know all these things, but somehow I keep forgetting them." Rather than forgetting them, I believe we simply do not know them because we were not taught them. At least that was our experiences during the years of formal religion in our lives until some years after our walk in the valley of divorce. So wherever you are in your walk of life, remember that transformation is the pinnacle of our inheritance blessings of abundance here on earth.

In closing, a real-world example of transformation is exemplified by the University of California Trojans football team of 2003–2004. This team was at a point where they were losing nearly every game in the Pacific-12 Conference until Coach Pete Carroll showed up. Even then, they were still losing games by a point or two and becoming frustrated with their lack of success. When asked how he turned it around, Coach Carroll answered, "I asked the team right before we were to play Oregon State if they believed that I believed that we can and will win. Not that *they* believed they could win, but that *I believed* that we could win." They all answered with a resounding, "Yes, we believe that you believe that we can and will win." Coach Carroll then said, "Well, then, ride on my belief until you get one of your own!"

USC went on to win every game except one in the 2003–2004 season and share in the National Championship. In the 2004–2005 season, they easily won another National Championship. In essence, that is what we are asking of you. "Do you believe that we believe these success principles and thought patterns really create success?" We hope you answered, "Yes," we believe that you believe! Well then, ride on our belief until you get one of your own. However, if you do not believe that God has an inheritance of abundance anointing you to prosperity and success, then may I have your portion?

Therefore, let us pray.

Heavenly Father, we believe that You believe in us and want to transform us from cursed to blessed. We believe that You believe Your inheritance given to us on earth (the blessings of abundance) will advance Your kingdom and glorify You at the appointed time and place when we use our talents and gifts. In Jesus' name, amen.

Think about It! Doesn't God want us to be transformed from cursed to blessed?

RECAP

Think about It! Isn't God glorified by the transformation of His children's success, protection, and prosperity of abundant blessing?

REMEMBER ...

Yes, God is most definitely glorified by his children's success, protection, and prosperity of abundant blessing! God has a purpose for us. God forgives us. God loves us forever. A life transformed is represented by the ability to set aside reality for a moment to dream beyond what is possible, and then experience it.

CONCLUSION

We started this book based on the promise of abundance by Jesus to all of His children in John 10:10. To put this statement in context, it is important to realize that this is the point in Jesus' ministry when He is finally telling everyone formally who He really is. He is the shepherd and the gatekeeper for His sheep. The Pharisees that were highly educated were His primary audience here. This is important because the analogy of shepherd and sheep are intentional and contentious. Sheep are uniquely stupid animals and perhaps the stupidest animal, or at least one of the most stupid. Sheep have a strong flocking instinct and fail to act independently of one another. Sheep follow. They do not lead. They have no offensive or defensive weapons (teeth, claws, etc.). They are slow to run away from danger and have low endurance. They cannot hide because they do not blend in to their surroundings. They are highly subtrainable. Ever see a sheep in a circus? No! Simply put, sheep are too stupid to train. So the analogy should be initially offensive to the Pharisees. Technically, it should be offensive to us too.

While some are smarter than others, humans in general are stupid. If fact, we'll bet there is not one person who can honestly say they have not done something stupid in their life. We certainly have. In fact, there is a book written about the stupidest things humans have done in history: *Stupid History* by Leland Gregory.

Here is just one of the stories we thought you would enjoy:

> In 1977, a woman called herself a "psychic escapologist" and announced she was going to drive a car sixty miles per hour over a course of one mile while wearing a blindfold … She crashed into the corner of a barn and was knocked unconscious and hospitalized for extensive injuries. Undaunted, she assured her fans that she would be able to escape from a large, heavy-duty plastic bag in only twenty minutes. The one thing this psychic escapologist couldn't escape was her own stupidity.

Now, you might be thinking that you have never done anything quite that stupid, but I think you get the point. Perhaps we can all identify with at least one joke from Jeff Foxworthy: "You might be a redneck if …" When compared with God, we are monumentally stupid no matter what our IQ is. And Jesus is trying to convey that message as He reveals himself formally.

The Pharisees believed that by their works (keeping the law), they would be assured entrance into heaven. Jesus was turning that belief upside down and saying, "No, that is not the way into heaven." Jesus was telling the Pharisees that the only way to heaven is by believing in Him (the gatekeeper). Then He will let His flock into the security of the pen/ gate. He was telling them that the Enemy will steal, kill, and destroy you if you are not protected by the shepherd, much like real predators of sheep (wolves, coyotes, etc.). Then He made a statement that He came to give life abundantly (more than we could ever ask or imagine) if we just believe.

The rest of John 10 concludes by saying that they (the audience of Pharisees) were divided. Some believed and others did not. The same holds true today! Either you believe that there is a promise of abundant life or not. If you are on the side of not believing, again may we have your portion of abundance? But before you decide, please review the prevailing themes of this book that are grounded in scriptural promises. We are sure you recognized them as you read along, but let's recap.

1. We all have a promise of joyful abundance that is part of our inheritance from our heavenly Father available to us here on earth.

2. We will choose to see and avoid our own limitations to God's abundant blessings/gifts.

3. We will not be surprised if the abundance we pray for comes in a different form than we asked or at a different time.

4. We will expect and embrace sufferings while knowing that growth occurs in the valleys and the mountaintops are worth the effort.

5. We will choose to keep the past in perspective and limit its power in our present through forgiveness.

6. We will learn to identify our unique talents/gifts and personality and use them in the natural expecting God to do the supernatural with them.

7. We will seek to know and become authentic man/woman and authentic marrieds in order to avoid the traps of conflict and divorce.

8. We will choose to think about what glorifies God and act accordingly, knowing that He is the only one who can ultimately answer *why*.

9. We will expect that there is an appointed time and place for reconciliation and redemption.

10. We will choose not to live according to the absolute doctrines

of performance or grace but recognize that balance between everything being a sin and nothing being a sin helps us avoid temptation consequences that limit blessings of abundance.

11. We will understand that we are four dimensional (biological, psychological, social, and spiritual) and seek health/improvement to facilitate transformation.

12. We will choose to believe there is significant meaning in 4 Abundant Life experiences grounded in four biblical truths.
    » We (children of God, Christ followers) are anointed to prosper,
    » At an appointed time and place,
    » When we use our talents and gifts
    » For the glory of Him!

The goal of this book is to help everyone recognize there are four biblical truths that allow us to experience a 4 Abundant Life. If we have done that, then we give it to the glory of Him who is able to do immeasurably more than we could ever ask or imagine. we will ask, imagine, and agree!

Matthew 18:19: "Again, truly I tell you that if two of you on earth agree about anything they ask for, it will be done for them by my Father in heaven."

References and Recommended Readings

[1]Fox, Emmet. (1989). *Sermon on the Mount: The Key to Success in Life.* San Francisco, CA: Harper.

[2]Hoehne, Ralph. (2008). *Anointed to Prosper.* Canada: Indigo Books and Music.

[3]Maxwell, John. (2009). *How Successful People Think.* New York, NY: Hachette Book Group.

[4]Carnegie, Dale. (1981). *How to Win Friends and Influence People.* New York, NY: Simon & Schuster.

[5]Tice, Lou. (2003). *Smart Talk: 5 Steps for Achieving Your Potential.* Seattle, WA: Pacific Institute Publishing. www.thepacificinstitute.com.

[6]Wilkinson, Bruce. (2000). *Prayer of Jabez.* Sisters, OR: Multnomah.

[7]Baker, Mark. (2007). *Jesus, the Greatest Therapist Who Ever Lived.* New York, NY: HarperCollins.

[8]Lucado, Max. (2001). *Traveling Light*. Nashville, TN: Thomas Nelson.

[9]Allen, James. (1902). *As a Man Thinketh*. Public Domain. www. asamanthinketh.com.

[10]Warner, Kurt. (2009). *All Things Possible*. New York, NY: HarperCollins.

[11]Osteen, Joel. (2012). *I Declare*. New York, NY: Faith Words.

[12]Osteen, Joel (2007). *Become a Better You*. New York, NY: Free Press.

[13]Frankl, Viktor. (1946). *Man's Search for Meaning*. Boston, MA: Beacon Press.

[14]Biro, Brian. (1997). *Beyond Success: The 15 Secrets to Effective Leadership and Life Based on Legendary Coach John Wooden's Pyramid of Success*. New York, NY: Perigee Books.

[15]McGraw, Phil. (2000). *Life Strategies: Doing What Works, Doing What Matters*. New York, NY: Hyperion.

[16]McGraw, Phil. (2001). *Self Matters: Creating Your Life from the Inside Out*. New York, NY: Free Press.

[17]Chapman, Gary. (2005). *The Four Seasons of a Marriage*. Wheaton, IL: Tyndale House.

[18]Tebow, Tim. (2011). *Through My Eyes*. New York, NY: HarperCollins.

[19]Dungy, Tony. (2007). *Quiet Strength: The Principles, Practices, & Priorities of a Winning Life*. Carol Stream, IL: Tyndale House.

[20]Osteen, Joel. (2009). *It's Your Time*. New York, NY: Simon & Schuster.

[21]Yancey, Philip. (1990). *Where Is God When It Hurts.* Grand Rapids, MI: Zondervan.

[22]Lucado, Max. (2002). *In the Eye of the Storm.* Nashville, TN: Thomas Nelson.

[23]Schuller, Robert. (2006). *Tough Times Never Last, But Tough People Do.* Nashville, TN: Thomas Nelson.

[24]Warren, Rick. (2003). *The Purpose Driven Life.* Grand Rapids, MI: Zondervan. http://www.purposedrivenlife.com/.

[25]Schuller, Robert. (1999). *Turning Hurts into Halos.* Nashville, TN: Thomas Nelson.

[26]Omartian, Stormie. (1997). *The Power of a Praying Wife.* Eugene, OR: Harvest House.

[27]Yancey, Philip. (2000). *Reaching for the Invisible God.* Grand Rapids, MI: Zondervan.

[28]Lucado, Max. (2012). *Grace.* Nashville, TN: Thomas Nelson.

[29]Dungy, Tony. (2010). *The Mentor Leader.* Carol Stream, IL: Tyndale House.

[30]Moore, Beth. (2010). *So Long Insecurity.* Chicago, IL: Tyndale House.

[31]Moore, Beth. (2007). *Breaking Free.* Nashville, TN: B & H Publishing.

[32]Osteen, Victoria. (2008). *Love Your Life.* New York, NY: Free Press.

[33]Wilkinson, Bruce. (2001). *Secrets of the Vine.* Sisters, OR: Multnomah.

[34]Carbonel, Mels. (1999). *Uniquely You Profile.* Blue Ridge, GA. www.myuy.com.

[35]Myers, Isabel Briggs; Mary H. McCaulley; Naomi Quenk; and Allan Hammer. (1998). *MBTI Handbook: A Guide to the Development and Use of the Myers-Briggs Type Indicator.* Consulting Psychologists Press, 3rd edition.

[36]Dobson, James. (2000). *Life on the Edge.* Nashville, TN: Thomas Nelson.

[37]Lewis, Robert. (2003). *The Quest for Authentic Manhood.* Nashville, TN: LifeWay Press.

[38]Love, Patricia and Steven Stosny. (2007). *How to Improve Your Marriage without Talking about It.* New York, NY: Three Rivers Press.

[39]Chapman, Gary. (2006). *Everybody Wins: The Chapman Guide to Solving Conflicts without arguing.* Wheaton, IL: Tyndale House.

[40]Becnel, Moe and Paige. (2009). *God Breathes on Blended Families.* Prairieville, LA: Blending A Family Ministry.

[41]Chapman, Gary. (2011). *Happily Ever After: Six Secrets to a Successful Marriage.* Wheaton, IL: Tyndale House.

[42]Kendrick, Stephen and Alex. (2008). *The Love Dare.* Nashville, Tennessee: The B & H Publishing Group.

[43]Eggerichs, Emerson. (2004). *Love and Respect.* Nashville, TN: Thomas Nelson.

[44]Chapman, Gary. (2010). *The Five Love Languages.* Chicago: Northfield Publishing.

[45]Chapman, Gary. (2006). *The Five Languages of Apology.* Chicago, IL: Northfield Publishing.

[46]Sacks, Peter. (2000). *Generation X Goes to College*. Chicago, IL: Open Court.

[47]American Psychiatric Association. (2000). *Diagnostic and Statistical Manual of Mental Disorders*, Fourth Edition, Text Revision (DSM-IV-TR).

[48]Walker, Lenoire. (1979). *The Battered Woman*. New York: Harper & Row.

[49]Palmer, Parker. (2007). *The Courage to Teach*. San Francisco, CA: John Wiley & Sons.

[50]Gardner, Richard. (1998). *The Parental Alienation Syndrome*. Cresskill, NJ: Creative Therapeutics.

[51]Richardson, Pamela. (2006). *A Kidnapped Mind: A Mother's Heartbreaking Story of Parent Alienation Syndrome*. Toronto, Canada: Dundurn Press.

[52]Baker, Amy (2007). *Adult Children of Parental Alienation Syndrome: Breaking the Ties That Bind*. New York, NY: Norton.

[53]Alexander, Debra Whiting. (2001). *Loving Your Teenage Daughter (Whether She Likes It or Not)*. Oakland, CA: New Harbinger Publications.

ABOUT THE AUTHORS

DR. ERIC OESTMANN, PHD, PT, is a professor, author, and professional speaker.

Eric Oestmann (pronounced *East-man*) is an internationally distinguished university educator with advanced degrees in health-care administration and management, research, and physical therapy. Dr. Oestmann began his career in the United States Air Force with numerous awards of meritorious service. Since 1995, he has been a licensed clinical physical therapist, and since 1997, he has engaged in health-care education programming and consulting services.

Dr. Eric is passionate about helping couples discover the biblical principles of authentic and abundant living and has been working with couples in churches and on college campuses coleading couples therapy and groups with Dr. Jo for more than nine years.

Dr. Eric has written twenty-four books/chapters related to health-care and education (Charles C. Thomas Publisher, VDM Publishing, Jones & Bartlett, and East-West Publishing), two screenplays, and nineteen research articles since 1995. Current research interests include blended families, authentic manhood and womanhood, parent alienation, and couples relational issues. He is also writing his third screenplay, which is entitled *Dancer's Image*.

DR. JOANNA OESTMANN, LMHC, LPC, LPCS, is a professor, author, and professional speaker. She is also a licensed mental health counselor and supervisor (LMHC) in Florida and is a licensed professional counselor (LPC) and supervisor (LPCS) in South Carolina. Additionally, she is a nationally certified psychologist, certified Florida Supreme Court mediator, and a certified neurolinguistic programming (NLP) technician, as well as a certified PREPARE/ENRICH relationship facilitator.

Dr. Jo has served as clinical supervisor and program director for psychological services at several mental health facilities and community mental health agencies and has worked as director of the department of psychiatry for Trident Regional Medical Center in Charleston, South Carolina, building skills in hospital administration, managed care, and medical services. Additionally, she has held a variety of clinical positions working with runaways, homeless women and children, disabled adults, pet bereavement and veterinary medicine, chronically mentally ill, bereavement and suicide prevention, domestic violence, rape trauma, and sexual abuse from a faith-based perspective integrating the mind, body, and spirit.

Dr. Jo's former faith-based private practice was in Holy Trinity

Episcopal Church in Clearwater, Florida, and part of The Samaritan Counseling Center of Tampa. This is an interfaith health-care ministry for people with emotional and stress-related issues to assist individuals, couples, and families by experienced and licensed professionals through counseling, education, and training, and consultation with clergy in the community. She added faith-based counseling services at Seacoast Church in Columbia, South Carolina, and now in her hometown at The Journey Church in Fernandina Beach, Florida.

Dr. Jo earned a doctorate degree in counseling psychology in 2000 from The University of Sarasota, specializing in medical psychology and gerontology. She also earned a master's degree in counseling psychology from Georgia State University, specializing in women's issues and sexuality in 1985. Her BA is in counseling from Eckerd College, and her AA is from Indian River College in psychology and education. She has published several journal articles as well as contributed to two counseling/health-care textbooks published by Jones and Bartlett and Pearson. Current research interests include blended families, authentic womanhood and manhood, parent alienation, and couples relational issues.

http://www.facebook.com/DrJoannaOestmannLmhcLpcLpcs
http://www.linkedin.com/pub/joanna-oestmann/2a/216/a46

Contact the authors to reserve a presentation, seminar, or other service related to experiencing the *4 Abundant Life* today!

Author Services

Individual, Couple Family, and Group Psychotherapy

Faith-based therapy focused on helping and healing the mind, body, and spirit. A cognitive-behavioral solution-focused approach grounded in biblical truths.

Authentic Womanhood/Manhood: A Partnership 4 Abundant Life

Dr. Jo and Dr. Eric are a husband and wife team counseling and educating couples, together for nine years, about leading authentic lives as men and woman reaching a partnership 4 Abundant Life. We have specific training in conjoint couples therapy and marriage repair. We know personally and professionally about the challenges of modern-day relationships. With this knowledge, we bring to conjoint couples' therapy a blend of female and male perspectives and a comfort with the issues common to evolving relationships. Both partners will learn practical and effective communication skills for better decision making, conflict resolution, and anger management. These interpersonal tools help you build a more satisfying and fulfilling collaborative relationship.

Your relationship success and health are our primary focus!

CONJOINT COUPLE THERAPY

The objective of conjoint couple therapy is to support the couple in their specific personal relationship goals, whatever they may be, while concurrently enhancing their relationship.

Conjoint couples therapy is a specialized form of couples' work that involves two therapists (a male and female) working closely with you and your partner to provide the balance and support you need to repair your relationship. The practice of conjoint couple therapy is active, purposeful, driving, and collaborative. It is the motivational model of couple happiness based on self-determination. The couple and therapists strive to develop and then implement a course of action and discovery that suits both partners. Because of the expectations and intensity, this therapy may not be for everyone. In the first (free) session, both therapists will meet with the couple and determine whether this course of action will be the most productive.

Drs. Jo and Eric help couples repair or enhance their relationships through conjoint couples counseling. Finding fulfillment and true partnership in a relationship is hard work. It starts with good communication, but it doesn't end there. Beyond communication, couples can benefit from identifying core issues and identifying core issues form the past and establishing a clear vision for the future. Additionally, learning each other's love languages and love language of apology, and by sharing deepest needs and desires by learning how to attend, acknowledge, and show empathy to each other, will be addressed with coping and anger management skills. Developing a couple's mission and vision statement for the relationship and contracts for relational, home, financial, and parenting for success helps couples focus on what they desire and how to achieve it as a team.

Key issues that can be strengthened are identified on the Marital Happiness Scale (MHS). Some common areas include marriage or remarriage, blended families, stepchildren, sibling abuse, sibling rivalry and the identified patient, separation and divorce, parent alienation, communication problems, not spending time together, lack of affection and appreciation, sex, finances, unemployment, arguing, time management, infertility, adoption, parenting, balancing your roles as partner and parent, infidelity, emotional or internet affairs, trust, depression and anxiety or mental illness, discontentment, in-laws and extended family relationships, chronic illness, domestic violence, emotional abuse, past sexual trauma, same-sex attraction, substance abuse, gambling, gaming, pornography, empty nest, grief and loss, developing spiritual intimacy, men becoming leaders and wives becoming encouragers, and having an intentional marriage.

Conjoint Couples Therapy: Two hours is the recommended session time to allow time for the issues to evolve.

What you will learn:

» How to make your marriage a priority and truly have a one-flesh relationship.

» How to fall more deeply in love.

» How to get your spouse to listen to you.

» How to resolve conflict.

» How to stop fighting about sex, money, kids, and extended family.

» How to dramatically improve your quality time and sex life.

» How to identify and communicate each other's love language.

» How to identify and communicate each other's language of apology.

Marathon Couples' Intensive Mini Retreat Therapy (eight hours)

Drs. Jo and Eric are also available for "Marathon Couples Therapy." This is a specific type of therapy that is short term and intensive. Its purpose is to help you resolve a crisis in your relationship. An assessment is done of the current crisis, and together goals are set to fit the time available. Eight hours is scheduled for this approach covered in one meeting, and weekend times are available.

You can expect individual time to share your story with one of the therapists as a comprehensive biopsychosocial assessment is completed, focusing on problems and strengths in your marriage. Evaluation of personal backgrounds and experiences, including your history as a couple together, will help identify unfinished business from the past that might be clouding or triggering issues today.

Acknowledgment of feelings, building emotional awareness, and enhancing skills in problem solving through effective communication is an opportunity to learn and experience how love and forgiveness can build through increased tolerance and through the recognition that personality and character differences can actually enhance your marriage and happiness.

A review of your love story; stages of marriage; marital plan past, present, and future; communication skills; problem-solving techniques; and how to be a team and winners in your relationship by changing misconceptions, reactions, stereotypes, prejudices, and self-defeating behaviors and irrational thoughts.

Upon completion of the therapy, we will prepare a written summary of your therapy process and recommendations for you as a couple, and if indicated, for each of you individually. Contracts for success help you carry the new things you learned into your daily routines.

PREPARE/ENRICH Certified Marital Enrichment of Premarital Counseling

Dr. Jo is a certified prepare/enrich counselor.

Prepare/Enrich is a program developed by Life Innovations, Inc. It is based upon a set of five inventories: Prepare (for premarital couples), Prepare-MC (for premarital couples with children), Prepare-CC (for cohabitating couples with or without children), Enrich (for married couples with or without children), and Mate (for couples over the age of fifty). These five inventories examine major relationship issues a couple may experience. The inventories include cover issues, such as communication, assertiveness, avoidance, self-confidence and self-esteem, deception, conflict resolution, personality, sexual expectations, financial issues, parenting, expectations with family of origin, extended family and friends, roles and vision of relationship, and ability to be flexible and open to change.

These inventories must be administered by a certified Prepare/Enrich counselor like Dr. Jo. Once couples complete their inventories, a number of counseling sessions are facilitated based upon the results. The sessions also include exercises designed to help improve relationship skills and to help the couple integrate the assessment results into their relationship experience.

The Prepare/Enrich program has six goals to strengthen the relationship bond and increase satisfaction.

» Explore relationship strengths and growth areas.

» Learn assertive communication and active listening skills.

» Learn how to resolve conflict using the Ten-Step model.

» Help the couple discuss their family of origin.

» Help the couple with financial planning and budgeting.

» Focus on personal, couple, and family goals.

PREPARE/ENRICH Assessment and Treatment Package

» Initial assessment with Dr. Jo.

» Sign up on Prepare/Enrich's website to obtain your personalized login information from Dr. Jo.

» Complete online assessment for both partners (thirty to forty-five minutes each).

» Follow-up sessions will be scheduled with Dr. Jo and Dr. Eric based on the individualized "couples report."

Workshops/Professional Speaking/Seminars

Dr. Jo and Dr. Eric offer workshops and seminars for ministry teams, helping professionals, schools, and the general public. Topics range from seminars like **4 Abundant Life, Authentic Womanhood/Manhood: The Partnership, Prepare/Enrich Facilitator Training** to seminars on compassion fatigue, burnout prevention, basic counseling skills, leadership skills, group facilitation, best practices for the classroom, learning styles, behavioral contracts, ethics, understanding and expressing grief, and creating an end-of-life celebration or memorial to leave a legacy that will last a life time.

Additionally, specialty seminars or trainings can be provided to your staff, congregation, or youth. Some examples of this are seminars on rape crisis and date rape, sexual abuse, stereotypes—the roles that bind us, giving and receiving, control issues, sexual restructuring for couples, keeping the romance alive, youth groups. There are also many topics for church staff such as Sunday school, youth organizations, and families that include topics such as: drug abuse, alcohol abuse, domestic violence, sexual perpetration, stress management and coping skills, problem solving and critical thinking, organizational management, communication skills, and others.

Seminars can be developed based on the needs of the organization, and we will work to identify skill gaps and recommend the best course of action to fill those gaps through professional development, program expansion, and on-site training.

MARITAL ENRICHMENT WORKSHOP WITH DRS. JOANNA AND ERIC OESTMANN

Successful Marriage Strategies to Live Happily Ever After

- » Explore relationship strengths and growth areas.
- » Learn assertive communication and active listening skills.
- » Learn how to resolve conflict using the Ten-Step model.
- » Help the couple discuss their family of origin.
- » Help the couple with financial planning and budgeting.
- » Focus on personal, couple, and family goals.

PET BEREAVEMENT AND BEYOND: CREATIVE CEREMONIES AND EXPRESSION OF GRIEF

Dedication: To all the pets—dogs and cats and all others—that have enriched our lives, given us unconditional love, and been there for us when no one else was: we love you and celebrate you always.

Audience: For families who have lost pets. How to help children and adults cope with the loss of a pet through creating meaningful ceremonies and creative memories.